# THE
# GREAT
# RESET

# THE
# GREAT
# RESET

## AND THE WAR FOR
## THE WORLD

# ALEX
# JONES

Skyhorse Publishing

Skyhorse Publishing books may be purchased in bulk at special discounts for sales promotion, corporate gifts, fund-raising, or educational purposes. Special editions can also be created to specifications. For details, contact the Special Sales Department, Skyhorse Publishing, 307 West 36th Street, 11th Floor, New York, NY 10018 or info@skyhorsepublishing.com.

Skyhorse® and Skyhorse Publishing® are registered trademarks of Skyhorse Publishing, Inc.', a Delaware corporation.

Visit our website at www.skyhorsepublishing.com.

10 9 8 7 6 5 4 3 2 1

Library of Congress Cataloging-in-Publication Data is available on file.

Cover design by Brian Peterson

Print ISBN: 978-1-5107-7404-9
Ebook ISBN: 978-1-5107-7405-6

Printed in the United States of America

# Contents

Forget the politicians. The politicians are put there to give you the idea that you have freedom of choice. You don't. You have no choice. You have owners. They own you. They own everything. They own all the important land. They own and control the corporations.

—George Carlin

Welcome to the year 2030. Welcome to my city—or should I say, "our city." I don't own anything. I don't own a car. I don't own a house. I don't own any appliances or any clothes.

It might seem odd to you, but it makes perfect sense for us in this city. Everything you considered a product, has now become a service. We have access to transportation, accommodation, food and all the things we need in our daily lives. One by one all these things became free, so it ended up not making sense for us to own much.

—*Forbes* magazine article by a World Economic Forum contributor in 2016 titled "Welcome to 2030: I Own Nothing, Have No Privacy, and Life Has Never Been Better"[1]

# THE
# GREAT
# RESET

## Chapter One

# What Is the Great Reset?

There's an eternal tension in the human soul between the desire for freedom and the desire to be told what to do by those in authority.

The human ability to work together in partnership is one of the great strengths of humanity, as is the ability to dissent from the accepted wisdom of the day. Many pollsters have noted the trend that, no matter the question, there's roughly a quarter of the population that will have an opposing view. Some have taken to calling it the idiot 25 percent of the population, and yet I see it as an evolutionary advantage, giving humanity unprecedented flexibility.

Let's imagine we're in a small tribe of about sixty people in the last Ice Age. Our leader, Thaag, tall, handsome, and a great warrior, suggests a certain route to the winter caves. It's the route the tribe has regularly used for the past several years.

But another member of the tribe, Uther, says, "There's been a lot of early snow, the glaciers are advancing, and I think that route will likely be blocked. Many might starve if we take that route. I know another route. It's a little longer, with some challenging terrain, but we'll definitely make it to the winter caves." Uther is known as the thinker of the tribe—maybe he's a medicine man—and sometimes he seems a little crazy, like when he starts talking about the spirits of the ancestors.

Many outcomes are possible.

Neither Thaag nor Uther knows the actual truth about which route makes the best sense.

Thaag and Uther might be enemies, with long-simmering rivalries. Thaag might demand the tribe take the traditional route, declaring that any who do not follow his decision should be banished from the tribe. Uther might respond that Thaag makes poor decisions, thus questioning his leadership of the tribe. Maybe there are ten to fifteen people who side with Uther, and they take the alternate, longer route to the winter caves. The group following Thaag all die, but the small band led by Uther survives. Maybe the group led by Uther, being much smaller in size, meets with another tribe who wipes them out.

The tribe survives, but, whether it is Thaag's or Uther's group that survives, the community is greatly weakened.

However, maybe Thaag and Uther are the best of friends, respecting the strengths of the other while also understanding the weaknesses. Uther understands that persuading Thaag is the best chance to ensure the survival of the greatest number of their people. And Thaag understands that some of Uther's crazy ideas have resulted in unprecedented success.

They talk and come up with a plan. They'll start the trek to the winter caves on the traditional route but send their fastest runners ahead to make sure the path is open. If the traditional route is blocked, at the early stages of the journey it will be easy to take a detour and switch to Uther's route.

That is how the strongest tribes are created, by talking through disagreements, and coming up with better plans.

This is not what we are doing in our world today.

* * *

For those readers who are more religiously minded, you might ask, What does the Bible say about the proper role between rulers and the people?

You might be surprised to learn that one of the earliest books of the Bible, the Book of Samuel, takes a very dim view of rulers, especially kings.

The Book of Samuel takes place after the Jews have fled Egypt in the Exodus and reestablished themselves in Israel. At this time, Israel had no king but instead had judges who would settle issues brought before them. This period was known as the Age of Judges and lasted about a century.

> In his old age Samuel appointed his sons judges over Israel. His first-born was named Joel, his second son, Abijah; they judged at Beer-sheba. His sons did not follow his example but sought illicit gain and accepted bribes, perverting justice. Therefore, all the elders of Israel came in a body to Samuel at Ramah and said to him, "Now that you are old, and your sons do not follow your example, appoint a king over us, as other nations have, to judge us."
>
> Samuel was displeased when they asked for a king to judge them. He prayed to the Lord, however, who said in answer, "Grant the people's every request. It is not you they reject, they are rejecting me as their king. As they have treated me constantly from the day I brought them from Egypt to this day, deserting me and worshipping strange gods, so do they treat you too. Now grant their request; but at the same time, warn them solemnly and inform them of the rights of the king who will rule over them."
>
> Samuel delivered the message of the Lord in full to those who were asking him for a king. He told them: "The rights of the king who will rule you will be as follows: He will take your sons and assign them to his chariots and horses, and they will run before his chariot. He will also appoint from among them his commanders of groups of a thousand and of a hundred soldiers. He will set them to do his plowing and harvesting, and to make his implements of war and the equipment of his chariots.

"He will use your daughters as ointment-makers, as cooks, and as bakers. He will take the best of your fields, vineyards, and olive groves, and give them to his officials. He will tithe your crops and your vineyards, and give the revenue to his eunuchs and his slaves. He will take your male and female servants, as well as your best oxen and asses, and use them to do his work. He will tithe your flocks and you yourselves will become his slaves. When this takes place, you will complain against the king whom you have chosen, but on that day the Lord will not answer you."[1]

A person might be forgiven if he comes to the conclusion that God was the original insurrectionist. However, the correct interpretation is that God was suspicious from the beginning that having a king, or any ruler, was a good idea. His preference was that the people kept Him in their hearts, and thus would not need any rulers.

When one uses the frame of the Samuel story, it becomes clear why many believe the United States to be a divinely ordained nation. Our founding documents clearly place the people as the true masters of our country, if only we act like it. The rulers serve the people, not the other way around. The more power is given to the people, the more God's will is accomplished. People who demand more freedom are working in God's interest, because they trust themselves to hear God's voice. The faithful are not fearful of the world around them. If you find a person filled with fear, then God is not with them.

The premise of this book is that the battle we are fighting against the Great Reset is nothing more than an ancient battle between the forces of freedom and tyranny. And yet, the critical piece of this fight is not found with those who are publicly advocating for our historic freedoms, or among those advocating for greater governmental control of your life.

The battle is won or lost by you, the public, deciding whether you want freedom over your life and decisions or more governmental control.

Choose wisely.

\* \* \*

Before we get to the Great Reset, we should ask the question, Who is its most well-known advocate?

That designation must surely belong to Klaus Schwab, founder and executive chairman of the World Economic Forum. This is how Schwab was described by Marc Benioff, chairman and CEO of the software company Salesforce, in the forward of Schwab's 2016 book, *The Fourth Industrial Revolution*:

> As the Founder and Executive Chairman of the World Economic Forum and its internationally renowned annual meeting in Davos, Switzerland, Klaus Schwab is uniquely placed to synthesize the experiences and views of leading global economic and technological experts, leaders of the world's largest businesses and the perspectives of government and civil society representatives into a panoramic view of the challenges ahead.[2]

That's a helpful piece of information. If you think the attendees at the World Economic Forum, held every year in Davos, Switzerland, have an accurate view of what's happening at the street and neighborhood level of their respective countries, you're likely to be impressed by Schwab's credentials. If you believe the wealthiest individuals of every country are somewhat clueless about what's genuinely going on in their countries, perhaps blinded by their expensive cars, enormous mansions, kids with drug problems, and private jets which spew an enormous amount of carbon into the atmosphere as they globe-trot every year to Davos, Switzerland, for the World Economic Forum, you're likely to be less impressed. Here's how Benioff finishes his introduction to Schwab's book:

> *The Fourth Industrial Revolution* is an important book for understanding the major trends shaping our world. It provides a way of thinking and analyzing the historic changes taking place

so that we can collectively create an empowering, prosperous, human-centered future for all. I am sure that you will gain valuable insights for navigating the future from reading this fascinating book.[3]

As I've reviewed Schwab's work, he reminds me of a stage magician, diverting your attention with one hand, so you don't see what he's doing with the other. It's easy to be fooled, as Schwab is comfortable with the kind of gee-whiz, ain't it cool, upbeat, pop psychology business books that were once so popular. One can view him as a well-trained persuader, but once you see the game he's playing, it's difficult to retain any respect for him.

The construction of the last paragraph of Benioff's introduction is a case in point. He tells you Schwab's book is important for "understanding the major trends shaping our world," as well as "thinking and analyzing the historic changes taking place."

You might find yourself being lulled into acceptance, thinking, *Yeah, I wouldn't mind reading a book about some important trends in our world.* But Schwab isn't interested in persuading you. He's interested in getting you to accept the plans of the richest and most powerful people in the world to make even more money and to have even more power over your life.

Benioff reveals the true intention of the book when he states that the purpose is to allow us to "collectively create an empowering, prosperous, human-centered future for all."

Really?

Do you think Marc Benioff or Klaus Schwab is genuinely interested in your opinions? The truth is they simply want us to be silent as they enact their plans.

Here's a reality check.

Have any members of the Davos Group come up to you in the past few years and said, "Hey, I really want to understand your life. Can we talk for a couple hours? I'll give you my email and cell phone number in case you think of something later."

I doubt it.

\* \* \*

Let's jump right into the words of Klaus Schwab, with the very first paragraph of the introduction to *The Fourth Industrial Revolution*. Schwab wrote:

> Of the many diverse and fascinating challenges we face today, the most intense and important is how to understand and shape the new technology revolution, which entails nothing less than a transformation of humankind. We are at the beginning of a revolution that is fundamentally changing the way we live, work, and relate to one another. In its scale, scope, and complexity, what I consider to be the fourth industrial revolution is unlike anything humankind has experienced before.[4]

Are you ready for an exciting journey, boys and girls? One almost expects Schwab to tell us how to get in touch with our sixth chakra and access our inner child. However, beneath the breathless, flowery language, he makes it crystal clear that this is about the "transformation of humanity." How does that strike you? Ready for the transformation? You probably didn't realize that was part of the deal.

The thorn of totalitarianism is hidden among the rose-colored language of Schwab. Can you find the thorn?

> We are witnessing profound shifts across all industries, marked by the emergence of new business models, the disruption of incumbents and the reshaping of production, consumption, transportation and delivery systems. On the societal front, a paradigm shift is underway in how we work and communicate, as well as how we express, inform, and entertain ourselves. Equally, governments and institutions are being reshaped, as are systems of education, healthcare, and transportation, among many others. New ways

of using technology to change behavior and our systems of production and consumption also offer the potential for supporting the regeneration and preservation of natural environments, rather than creating hidden costs in the forms of externalities.[5]

Let's count the number of subtle calls to increased control over your life contained in that single paragraph. We've got the "profound shifts across all industries," which will lead to the "disruption of incumbents and reshaping of production, consumption, transportation and delivery systems." And let's not forget the blatant lies they tell, like leading you to believe they want incumbents to be disrupted.

They're the incumbents.

They're doing this so they don't get disrupted. They want a front row seat, with their hand on the wheel, as they reshape "production, consumption, transportation, and delivery systems."

Then Schwab moves to the "societal front" where he breathlessly informs us that "a paradigm shift is underway in how we work, communicate, as well as how we express, inform, and entertain ourselves." Again, let's note the subtle persuasion. It's already happening, he wants you to think, almost like the guy who pesters a woman for a dinner date, then when she finally agrees, says, "Would you like to have sex before or after dinner?" How much does Schwab and his gang intend to control? Just how you work, communicate, express, inform, and entertain yourself. The one frontier where you may still have some level of control is your thoughts, but they're probably just waiting for Elon Musk to perfect his Neuro-Link device, so they've got a straight shot into your brain.

Next, he moves to the institutions: "Equally, governments and institutions are being reshaped as are systems of education, healthcare, and transportation, among many others." Let's put that into the plain person translator, and we conclude they just want to control the schools, the medical system, and your freedom of movement. You can't say that Schwab and his gang aren't ambitious.

And what do Schwab and company actually want? Well, helpfully, they tell us: "New ways of using technology to change behavior and our systems of production and consumption also offer the potential for supporting the regeneration and preservation of natural environments." They're the ones who want to use technology to reshape us, as well as control the means of production and consumption. In other words, you'll eat our plant-based burgers and lab-grown meat when we tell you.

This may sound like a minor point, but Schwab is a really bad writer.

However, I think Schwab's writing and persuasion skills lie at the heart of this book. One can make the argument that all writing is about persuasion. But the quality of the writing is determined by the quality of the author's thinking. Brilliant writing is the result of a brilliant mind. The most engaging writing is generally the result of the author being willing to explore provocative ideas in a way the reader may not have considered before picking up the book.

Schwab is a ham-handed persuader, always relying on the same three-pronged approach.

First, use a lot of flowery, gee-whiz, isn't progress amazing sections with some interesting facts of which the reader might not be aware.

Second, introduce some threat such as instability of the system, to make people uneasy.

Third, let the reader know that Schwab and his Davos Group have the answer.

This is generally known in persuasion as the problem, reaction, solution dynamic.

* * *

It's said we don't think in facts, but in narratives. If we have a compelling narrative, we will subconsciously dismiss facts that don't fit the narrative and give greater weight to those that do fit the narrative. Schwab is VERY interested in giving you the narrative for his plan:

The changes are so profound, from the perspective of human history, there has never been a time of greater promise or potential peril. My concern, however, is that decision makers are too often caught in traditional, linear (and nondisruptive) thinking or too absorbed by immediate concerns to think strategically about the forces of disruption and innovation shaping our future.[6]

Understanding the persuasion game is probably one of the most important things you will learn in this book. If somebody wants you to make BIG changes, they need to convince you that the problem is also BIG.

Schwab would have you believe that "The changes are so profound, from the perspective of human history, there has never been a time of greater promise or peril." Would any reputable historian agree with that statement? How about World War II? The Cuban Missile Crisis, when the United States and the Soviet Union stood on the brink of nuclear war? The Black Death in Europe of the fourteenth century, which killed an estimated seventy-five to two hundred million people?

Schwab is clearly using exaggerated language (outright lies) to convince you to follow his suggestions. In real life, when somebody lies to you, you stop listening to them. However, we're going to go even deeper to reveal the extent of Schwab's deceptions and the true plans of his Davos Group.

After his clearly inflated claim about the "promise and peril" of our current time, Schwab moves to breaking down the defenses of those who might frustrate his plans when he writes, "My concern, however, is that decision makers are too often caught in traditional, linear (and nondisruptive) thinking or too absorbed by immediate concerns to think strategically about the forces of disruption and innovation."

Let's translate Schwab's flowery language into its true meaning.

Those currently in charge are too stupid to understand the brilliance of my plan! Stand aside, peasants, and let me unleash my massive brainpower on the world! (Insert maniacal supervillain laugh.) Honestly, is there any other way to understand the condescension in Schwab's writing?

Near the end of the introduction of the book, Schwab lays out his vision of how this transformation will take place:

> The fundamental and global nature of this revolution means it will affect and be influenced by all countries, economies, sectors and people. It is, therefore, critical that we invest attention and energy in multi-stakeholder cooperation across academic, social, political, national and industry boundaries. These interactions and collaborations are needed to create positive, common, and hope-filled narratives, enabling individuals and groups from all parts of the world to participate in, and benefit from, the ongoing transformations.[7]

This is not a revolution that is starting at the grass roots among the proletariat. This is a revolution starting in the corporate suites, among the bourgeoisie, where transnational business people get together at big meetings in places like Davos, Switzerland.

Are we to believe this is genuinely being done in the name of the people?

Because I'm pretty certain the average person has no idea what "multi-stakeholder cooperation" means. And does the average person go to bed at night worrying about the need to "create positive, common, and hope-filled narratives"?

This book will detail all parts of Schwab's strategy to use the Great Reset to achieve an unprecedented amount of control over your daily life. This genuinely is a "war for the world." It is a war to control the future of human development and capture control of the human species. We all have a vital stake in the outcome. I freely confess that in this book I use abundant satire and mockery. And yet that's not to imply that the plans of Schwab and the Davos Group are not dangerous. I absolutely believe they are planning an enormous assault on our freedoms, and we must figure out the best way to counter their designs.

A power the elites have used for thousands of years is respect and reverence. In previous centuries we were encouraged to believe our rulers were descendants of the gods, or some type of advanced human being. I use satire and mockery to demonstrate Schwab and his minions do not deserve your respect or deference.

Our enemies are human and possess no more strength or intelligence than you do. They currently possess many of the levers of power, whether in the media, government, or finance, but eventually they are accountable to the common people.

You are the ones who will decide whether the future is one of freedom and prosperity, or bondage and suffering.

The power is in your hands.

*Chapter Two*

# Developing the System of Control

Perhaps it's because Klaus Schwab released his first book, *The Fourth Industrial Revolution*, in 2016, with the expectation of a Hillary Clinton win of the presidency, but instead got Donald Trump, that Schwab didn't get the world to pay attention to the ideas in his book.

Maybe that's why in 2018 he published his second book, *Shaping the Future of the Fourth Industrial Revolution*, which he was hoping might have a greater impact. It's like Margaret Mitchell publishing *Gone with the Wind* in 1936, not having it become a massive bestseller, then coming back a few years later with the sequel, *Really Gone with the Wind*.

I imagine Schwab hanging out among all his rich friends in Davos, Switzerland, scratching his head and saying, "Why didn't Hillary win?" and "I don't know a single person who voted for Donald Trump." Maybe like Hillary after 2008 when she got blown away by Barack Obama, Schwab said, "Well, let's give it another try."

*Maybe the problem was with Marc Benioff and his foreword*, Schwab thinks. *Yeah, Salesforce is a big company in San Francisco and all the Silicon Valley people know about it, but maybe I need a bigger name. Let me think. Oh, I've got it! How about Microsoft? I'll get their CEO, Satya Nadella. That will make people stand up and take notice. Bill Gates founded Microsoft, and everybody loves Bill Gates.*

However, Nadella doesn't do much better than Benioff. Nadella begins by worshipping at the altar of Schwab and the World Economic Forum with this cringeworthy opening:

> Through insightful convenings and publishing, the World Economic Forum and its founder, Klaus Schwab, have continued to cast a bright light on both the opportunities and the challenges of the Fourth Industrial Revolution. They are right to confront zero-sum thinking about the coming wave of new technologies by pointing out that their evolution is entirely within our power.[1]

If you're wondering much about Satya Nadella, the bottom of the first page of the foreword gives you a quick little information bite: Satya Nadella is CEO of Microsoft and author of *Hit Refresh: The Quest to Rediscover Microsoft's Soul and Imagine a Better Future for Everyone.*[2] Do you ever wonder why all these business types often use religious language in their writing, when they probably don't have much religion in the first place? Don't get me wrong. I'm all in favor of business leaders talking about business. I just think it's probably a good idea to stay in that lane.

As I read these books, many of the so-called business leaders strike me as nothing more than overachieving high school students who want to show the principal how much better they understand the school than anybody else. Then, when the principal is sufficiently impressed, ask to be appointed to student council, rather than go through the messy work of being elected by the student body. Here's a sample of this thinking from Nadella:

> The confluence of data with massive computational storage and cognitive power will transform industry and society at every level, creating opportunities that were once unimaginable from health and education to agriculture, manufacturing and services. My company and others are betting on the convergence of several important technology shifts—mixed reality, artificial

intelligence, and quantum computing. With mixed reality we are building the ultimate computing experience, one in which your field of view becomes a computing surface; your digital world and your physical world become one. The data, apps, and even the colleagues and friends on your phone or tablet will be available anywhere you want to access them—while you're working in your office, visiting a customer, or collaborating with colleagues in a conference room.[3]

I don't mean to denigrate the technological achievements of companies like Microsoft. It's simply that I think they've overstated their value to the average person. Let's take the idea that your apps can go with you on your phone or laptop.

That's great.

Maybe I can go to a conference, get up an hour or two early, and do a little work on my laptop or check emails on my phone. However, I still probably need to hit the gym, take a shower, get some coffee, and get something to eat before the first speaker takes the stage at 9 a.m. Thanks to Big Tech I can do a little more work in my day.

But I don't think that calls for a reordering of society. I still have to get my ass down to the gym and pedal my six miles if I want to have the slightest bit of health benefit. And if by chance, I'm staying in a nice hotel and the bike at the gym has a screen that shows a video of bicycling through the French countryside as I pump my legs, well, that's all nice and good. But just because I've seen a little of the French countryside while I'm sweating on the bike doesn't mean I have any increased appreciation or understanding of French culture.

Like Schwab, Nadella wants to dazzle you with the technological changes, because if you're a little intimidated, it makes you easier to control. You won't raise your hand to ask a question because you don't want to sound stupid. Maybe that's my superpower. I don't mind sounding stupid. (And don't you always remember your teachers saying, "There's no such thing as a stupid question"?)

But when they can't answer my stupid questions, well, who's the stupid one? Here's Nadella, hoping you'll feel intimidated and hand power over to Klaus Schwab and his Davos buddies:

> Similarly, industry and society must come together to focus on empowering both people and organizations by democratizing access to intelligence to help solve our most pressing challenges. For example, if AI is one of technology's top priorities, healthcare is surely one of AI's most urgent applications. Coupled with mixed reality, the cloud and business optimization tools, AI will be central to health care transformation under way on the science bench, in the clinic and throughout medical center operations.[4]

That paragraph certainly wasn't put together by somebody with the slightest bit of liberal arts training. It makes me wonder if they've ever read a book that held their attention. Okay, so Nadella writes, "industry and society must come together" for the purpose of "democratizing intelligence." Why in God's name do industry and society have to come together for the purpose of democratizing intelligence, whatever the hell that means? Does some homeless person in Los Angeles hold one of the hidden keys to artificial intelligence? Is there some third grader in Wisconsin who, if we could just get her to accept the need to "democratize intelligence," all would be good in the world?

All right, I accept that good healthcare is a priority. What do we know about good health? Don't be overweight. Eat a healthy diet. Exercise. Have good social relationships. On that last point, good social relationships, I suggest you read what Malcolm Gladwell has written about their importance in a short essay titled "The Roseto Mystery." Here's the anomaly about this small Pennsylvania town, first noticed by a man named Stewart Wolf in the 1950s:

> Wolf was a physician. He studied digestion and the stomach and taught in the medical school at the University of Oklahoma.

He spent his summers on a farm in Pennsylvania, not far from Roseto—although that, of course, didn't mean much, since Roseto was so much in its own world that it was possible to live in the next town and never know much about it. "One of the times when we were up there for the summer—this would have been in the late nineteen fifties—I was invited to give a talk at the local medical society," Wolf said several years later in an interview. "After the talk was over, one of the local doctors invited me to have a beer. And while we were having a drink, he said, 'You know, I've been practicing for seventeen years. I get patients from all over, and I rarely find anyone from Roseto under the age of sixty-five with heart disease.'"[5]

This was a shocking finding to Wolf, as in the late 1950s, heart attacks were the leading cause of death for men under the age of sixty-five. How could heart attacks be so rare in this small Pennsylvania town, populated mainly by immigrants from a small town in southern Italy? The researchers looked at genetics, food, and exercise and could find no correlation. Then they started looking at the social structure of the town itself:

> What Wolf began to realize was that the secret of Roseto wasn't diet or exercise or genes or location. *It had to be Roseto itself.* As Bruhn and Wolf walked around the town, they figured out why. They looked at how Rosetans visited one another, stopping to chat in Italian on the street, say, or cooking for one another in their backyards. They learned about the extended family clans that underlay the town's social structure. They saw how many homes had three generations living under one roof, and how much respect grandparents commanded. They went to mass at Our Lady of Mount Carmel and saw the unifying and calming effects of the church. They counted twenty-two separate civic organizations in a town of just under two thousand people.[6]

But Nadella doesn't want to talk about things like a good weight, healthy diet, exercise, and positive social relationships. Instead, he wants to talk about "individual variability in genes, immunological systems, and lifestyle for each person." All of those are worthy subjects of study, but why does that require us to reorder our society into some Technocratic theocracy?

And where is there any discussion about the quality of our social connections? How many people do we interact with in a positive way during a typical day? The world Schwab and Nadella want to create is devoid of these connections and as a result might be the unhealthiest society ever devised by the mind of man.

Finally, Nadella moves to the close, which is where he wants to disarm the people of their skepticism. Because if you trust them, you'll let them do things you wouldn't otherwise let them do:

> Finally, trust in today's digital world means everything. In every corner of this world, we need a revitalized regulatory environment that promotes innovative and confident use of technology. The biggest problem is antiquated laws that are ill-suited to deal with contemporary problems.
>
> The prescient topics explored in this book, coupled with the dialogue it sparks at World Economic Forum gatherings, are vital contributions to understanding and solutions. The potential benefits are unprecedented, and as this book concludes, public-private leadership are essential.[7]

Nadella is a smart man. He didn't get to his position at Microsoft by being an idiot.

Maybe he got there by being a "yes man," but certainly not because he wasn't smart. Like any good general, he understands the strengths and weaknesses of his own side, as well as those of his enemy. Nadella understands that his side has these technological wonders created by his engineers. That is a great advantage.

What Nadella realizes he lacks is support for a great restructuring of society.

In order to implement his plans, he needs to get you to "trust" him. Think about trust in your own life. Many Catholics have been horrified in recent years to learn of the sexual abuse of children by trusted members of the clergy. In hindsight, the trust these parents placed in their clergy members is difficult to understand. However, these were supposed to be men and women of God who lived in fear of their eternal souls. It was difficult for many to reconcile this idea with the wickedness of some supposed people of God.

Trust is not something we give people in the absence of a robust system of transparency and accountability. There have been too many examples in history when trust has been misplaced. Nadella wants to repeat the mistakes of the past when he writes, "The biggest problem is antiquated laws that are ill-suited to deal with contemporary problems."

Could you imagine the government creating a new childcare program, where they told you that you couldn't observe the facilities, or examine the credentials of the people running the facility? Parents would stage a revolt.

But Nadella just wants you to trust him with these technological changes.

Like Schwab, Nadella wants to close the deal with you, promising the enormous benefits, while downplaying the risks. Because if they need to get your consent, they're not going to tell you about the club they've got hidden behind their back if you protest. The hidden club is contained in the sentence "The potential benefits are unprecedented, and as this book concludes, public-private leadership and partnership are essential."

Here's the perspective I'm going to take about this sentence. Every time you hear the expression "public-private" or "partnership," I want you to replace it with the word "fascism." Because you see, fascism, as practiced in both Mussolini's Italy and Hitler's Germany, was a public-private partnership. This is how fascism differs from communism.

The communists seized the means of production and tried to run these industries. They didn't do a good job.

Mussolini and Hitler had a different idea.

Government and big business were both powerful entities. A battle between these two groups would be unproductive, as communists found out to their dismay. But instead of a fight, a cunning leader might understand that a deal could be made. Big business leaders don't like workers who agitate for better working conditions and higher pay. As a first step, Mussolini and Hitler broke the labor unions. Once the workers were disarmed, the leaders were free to attack other countries and do what they wanted with their own dissidents.

Whenever you hear the word "public-private," I want you to translate it into your mind as a promise that the government will not hesitate to attack the people if they protest against the plans of Big Business.

\* \* \*

In the preface to his second book, Schwab also begins by talking about trust. The cloaked language he uses makes one wish to have been a fly on the wall among the Davos elite when Trump was elected in 2016 and the years that followed. They must have been falling all over themselves wondering whether Trump and his skepticism were the disease, or simply a symptom of something much larger that threatened to undermine their plans:

> Public trust in business, government, the media and even civil society has fallen to the point where more than half of the world feels the current system is failing them. The widening gap in trust between those in the country's top income quartile and the rest of the population indicates that social cohesion is fragile at best, and very close to breaking down at worst.
>
> It is this precarious political and social context that we face both the opportunities and the challenges of a range of powerful, emerging technologies—from artificial intelligence, to

biotechnologies, advanced materials to quantum computing—
that will drive radical shifts in the way we live, and which I have
described as compromising the Fourth Industrial Revolution.[8]

In the middle of the first Trump term, Schwab and his Davos crew
must have been nervous. According to Schwab, the bottom 75 percent of the country thinks the top 25 percent is screwing them. They
understood that things were very close to falling apart, which is why
he wrote, "social cohesion is fragile at best." This isn't me talking. This
was Klaus Schwab in 2018.

But Schwab is nothing if not persistent. He was still pushing this
Fourth Industrial Revolution when he wrote, "we face both the opportunities and the challenges of a range of powerful, emerging technologies." He's like that Catholic priest who says to the parents of his
parish, "I know there's been a lot of accusations about priests being
alone with kids, but I still want to take your young teenage boys away
for a long ski weekend."

Schwab freely admits that the elite of the world are not trusted by
the vast majority of the population, but he's going to keep going:

> But standing at these crossroads means we bear a huge responsi-
> bility. If we miss this window of opportunity to shape new tech-
> nologies in ways that promote the common good, enhance human
> dignity and protect the environment, there is a good chance that
> the challenges we experience today will only be exacerbated, as
> narrow interests and biased systems further entrench inequalities
> and compromise the rights of people in every country.[9]

The audacity of Schwab is genuinely breathtaking. The Davos group
members are the elite 1 percent of the world. If there has been a problem with income inequality, human dignity, or degradation of the
environment, it's the fault of that 1 percent.

It's a little like the main suspect in a murder being the detective
of the crime. That might make for an interesting movie but should

always remain in the realm of fiction. Those who caused these problems should not be driving the solution. Schwab lets you know that his brain trust he relies on are the very people who created this mistrust among the population:

> This book is the product of many world-class experts from across the World Economic Forum's diverse community. Section 2, in particular, synthesizes the perspectives of leading thinkers from the Forum's Global Future Councils and Expert Network. Were it not for their generous contributions of time and knowledge, it would have been impossible to cover the breadth of subject matter to the depth required to make sense of the most impactful technology domains. I also very much appreciate the thoughtful and most relevant reflections provided by Satya Nadella in the foreword.[10]

These are people who don't live in your world. These are ivory tower intellectuals, bought and paid for by the corporate titans who are upset that they don't yet have complete control over your world.

But they don't call it corruption.

They call it "partnership."

While he sets out much of the same argument in the introduction as he does the preface, Schwab tells you exactly what he hopes to bring about at the end of his introduction.

> The book closes with a vision for systems leadership, summarizing the critical governance issues that leaders from all sectors, along with the general public, must tackle together to create an inclusive, sustainable, and prosperous future.[11]

Schwab isn't inviting you to help him create a better future. He's inviting you to help him build your prison cell.

\* \* \*

In his second book, Schwab seemed to believe he had to simplify his original message, so that at the end of each chapter, he provided a simple one-to-two-page summary.

The first question he seeks to answer is to define the Fourth Industrial Revolution. Here is how Schwab describes it in his chapter "Framing the Fourth Industrial Revolution":

> The Fourth Industrial Revolution is a way of describing a set of ongoing and impending transformations in the systems that surround us, and which most of us take for granted every day. While it may not feel momentous to those of us experiencing a series of small but significant adjustments to life on a daily basis, it is not a minor change—the Fourth Industrial Revolution is a new chapter in human development, on par with the first, second, and third Industrial revolutions, and once again driven by the increasing availability and interaction of a set of extraordinary technologies.[12]

Confused?

Schwab is telling you that the public doesn't see these momentous changes. Sure, the people notice some minor changes, but things are genuinely moving in a big way, according to Schwab. Once again, Schwab and his Davos group are just so much better at figuring out what's happening in your life than you.

And Schwab doesn't want you depending on yourself to figure out these changes, or any of the local or national institutions you've relied on for years. In a rhetorical sleight of hand that would have done the communists proud as they established their Young Pioneer program to indoctrinate the children, Schwab reveals his plan in a section titled "A New Leadership Mindset":

> These three challenges—distributing benefits, managing externalities and ensuring a human-centered future—cannot be easily solved top-down through regulation or well-meaning government

initiatives. Nor is it at all likely that the current constellation of international and national institutions, market structures, organized and spontaneous social movements and incentives for individuals will lead to powerful new technologies being widely available, completely free from harm and fully focused on empowering the people that use them.[13]

This should strike everybody as a shot across the bow of any person who believes in a civil and peaceful society. Schwab has no interest in typical government programs. He doesn't believe in any currently existing international or national institutions. Neither does he believe in any spontaneous social movements or individuals who rise up with good ideas or any of the typical incentive programs that might bring about positive change. Schwab and his Davos gang are interested in wiping out every one of the previously existing social structures that have guided the development of countries and nations.

I've always believed that if somebody confesses something disturbing about themselves, such as "I've never been able to be faithful," you should pay attention. If you choose to date that person, then find your heart broken when they cheat on you, the blame should fall on you.

Schwab makes it clear he intends to wipe away the power of all our institutions and structures. In the chapter summary, Schwab lays it out again:

> The Fourth Industrial Revolution is a new chapter in human development, driven by the increasing availability and interaction of a set of extraordinary technologies, building on three previous technological revolutions. This revolution is only in its early stages, which provides humankind with the opportunity and responsibility to shape not just the design of new technologies, but also more agile forms of governance and positive values that will fundamentally change how we live, work, and relate to each other.[14]

What are these "more agile forms of governance"? A summary execution by firing squad without the benefit of a trial? Maybe the continued illegal detention of January 6, 2021, protestors, many of whom languish in jails more than a year after the event, who have been denied a speedy trial?

And there really isn't much discussion of what these "positive values" are, except for the concern that the 75 percent of the country mentioned before doesn't seem to trust the top 25 percent. Are the members of the Davos group or Karl Schwab going to come to your house and ask, "Why don't you like me?"?

It's likely that Schwab's plan involves pledging your "trust" to the Davos group, lest you suffer the punishments made possible by their more "agile" forms of governance.

After all, how are they going to get you to accept these fundamental changes to "how we live, work, and relate to each other?"

What will be done to those who object?

Schwab is curiously silent on such subjects.

\* \* \*

For a long portion of his second book, Schwab spends a great deal of time talking about the interconnectedness of technology, as if we didn't realize that "The technologies of the Fourth Industrial Revolution are connected to one another in that they all require and build on the digital capabilities and networks created by the third Industrial Revolution, just as those technologies required and built on the electricity networks of the second Industrial Revolution."[15]

That's almost as self-evident as saying, "Before they could be your parents, your grandparents needed to have children." It is at such banalities that Schwab excels.

In the next chapter, Schwab discusses the "politics of technologies," and what he calls the mistaken twin beliefs that "technology drives history" and that "technology is value neutral."[16] In fact, he labels both beliefs "extremely dangerous."[17] If you were looking for at least one area of life where politics didn't intrude, Schwab will give you no sanctuary. It's Schwab's belief that "When any technology is created, it contains the residue of values, goals and compromises. And the more powerful the technology, the more important it becomes to appreciate what these are."[18]

Perhaps he's right.

Maybe if people understood that Mark Zuckerberg created Facebook as a way for his fellow Harvard males to rate the attractiveness of the Harvard females, we'd all resign from the platform, Zuckerberg would lose all of his money, and he would end up as a homeless person sleeping on the streets of San Francisco. I understand it's a long shot, but a person can dream.

One must be wary of how Schwab and his Davos group use language.

I think one of the most dangerous words that should concern you is "stakeholder." This is how Schwab ends the chapter titled "Empowering All Stakeholders":

> Creating a prosperous, inclusive and equitable Fourth Industrial Revolution for society and citizens means being conscious of the choices we make in technological systems which will inevitably impact economic, environmental and social systems. This means having the courage to confront existing economic and political paradigms and reshaping them to empower individuals regardless of ethnicity, age, gender or background.[19]

Our country was founded on the idea of individual rights. The government is supposed to protect those rights. That's called freedom.

But if Schwab and company come up with a way to short-circuit those rights, that would be a powerful tool. This is the definition of "stakeholder" from Investopedia:

A stakeholder is a party that has an interest in a company and can either affect or be affected by the business. The primary stakeholders in a typical corporation are its investors, employees, customers, and suppliers.

However, with the increasing attention on corporate social responsibility, the concept has been extended to include communities, governments, and trade associations.[20]

Whenever you hear the word "stakeholder," you should think of it as a weapon Schwab and company will use to deprive a person of their rights.

* * *

Section 2 of Schwab's second book is titled "Technologies, Opportunities and Disruption" and contains a great deal of unrelated material such as this gem:

The rising importance and applicability of machine learning has created the demand for new types of customized computing architectures. Google, one of the world's largest purchasers of chips, designed large numbers of tensor processing units, application-specific integrated circuits designed for deep learning algorithms.[21]

One might be tempted to discount the importance of such a bland paragraph, except for how it slips in the idea of "deep learning algorithms." Remember all those science fiction machines you saw as a kid where the robot went crazy, killing people, and the climax of the film was when the hero discovered it wasn't the robot that was at fault, but the psychologically deranged developer? Yeah, this is one of those kinds of problems. Except that instead of the robot going on a killing spree, the algorithm will simply declare your well-reasoned policy disagreement to be "hate speech" or, even worse, "racist." Yes, the problem is not the machine; it's the person who programmed it. Which is why the radical leftists of Silicon Valley are so distrusted by the rest of America. The next section is titled "The Internet of Things" and comes to the shocking conclusion that much of our world is interconnected. Another section, "Cyber Risks," comes to the inspired realization that there are "cyber risks" involved in technology and we should spend money to defend against these risks. Final chapters on artificial intelligence, biotechnologies, drones, advanced materials, and virtual reality are similarly unenlightening. It's only when we get to the conclusion of Schwab's second book that he starts to reveal how he and his Davos Group are going to restructure society. Don't worry, he tells you. We won't just have governments or corporations coming after you; there will be other sources of pressure:

> Governance, however, is not just government: the formal structures we have for creating laws and regulations. Governance includes the development and use of standards, the emergence of social norms that can constrain or endorse use, private incentive schemes, certification and oversight by professional bodies, industry agreements and the policies that organizations apply voluntarily or by contract in their relationship with competitors, suppliers, partners and customers.[22]

In this world that Schwab wants to create, you'll have to worry about more than just government. In truth, it doesn't seem as if Schwab has much use for government, unless it does exactly what he wants. Instead, Schwab is counting on the big corporations to function as de facto governments, possibly through their terms of service. Does it make sense how the Big Tech companies were able to censor conservative viewpoints in the run-up to the 2020 election? How did they do this when this violated the spirit of our First Amendment? How did these tech leaders justify it to their conscience? Possibly because they'd been brainwashed by Klaus Schwab at all those Davos Conferences?

And did you notice how Schwab pushes the "emergence of social norms" probably by the use of his beloved "conversations," which are nothing more than scripts developed by Schwab's chosen actors, as if we were watching a Broadway play? But with Schwab's scripts, the fiction becomes reality.

If you're wondering how these new standards are going to be developed, don't worry. They'll be developed by the "experts":

> Communities of professionals are essential for establishing the right standards—especially standards that reflect a consensus of values and stakeholder priorities. The IEEE, for example, draws on 423,000 members to build consensus among organizations and deliver safety, reliability and interoperability in a range of electrical and digital systems. Their guidelines for AI show that they are thinking through the broad impact of technologies and not just focusing on the technical requirements or compliance."[23]

Is it becoming clear there's never going to be an actual vote? Instead, there's going to be a managed discussion with a predetermined outcome, amenable to that of Schwab and his Davos friends.

In his advice for governments, Schwab tells governments they must adopt "agile governance," which he defines as:

> [A]n essential strategy to adapt how policies are generated, deliberated, enacted and enforced to create better governance outcomes in the Fourth Industrial Revolution. Inspired by the Agile Manifesto and a report by the World Economic Forum Global Agenda Council on the Future of Software and Society, the concept of agile governance seeks to match the nimbleness, fluidity, flexibility and adaptiveness of the technologies themselves and the private-sector actors adopting them.[24]

Just in case you wonder what all that means, it means that Schwab wants to act with all of the ethics of our largest corporations, who have

polluted our air and water, the pharmaceutical companies who clamor
for complete financial immunity for their vaccines, and the Big Tech
who never seem to suffer for violating American values of free speech
and free competition. Schwab goes on to detail what some of these
models might look like when he writes:

- Encouraging collaborations between governments and businesses
  to create "developtory sandboxes" and "experimental testbeds"
  to develop regulations using iterative, cross-sectoral and flexible
  approaches as discussed by Geoff Mulgan . . .
- Promoting the development of ecosystems of private regulators,
  competing in markets to deliver governance in line with
  overarching social goals, as proposed by Gillian Hadfield in *Rules
  for a Flat World.*[25]

These proposals are a blueprint for disaster. If liberals of the 1970s were
terrified of the power of the intelligence agencies, the defense industry,
and big business, those concerns were nothing compared to the corpo-
rate-based power world envisioned by Schwab.

I'm not sure any filmmaker or writer has adequately captured the
dystopian elements of this planned future. The closest comparison I
can make is to the *Alien* movies, in which a corporation partners with
the government to bring a monster back to Earth to study its unique
biology. This is a genuinely lawless future in which the only justice
meted out is that given by powerful corporations.

Let's understand the magic show with which Schwab hopes to dazzle the public.

He goes into minute and exquisite detail about all the advances in
technology and summarizes many of the questions raised by these new
technologies.

At the same time we're supposed to be dazzled by these advances,
he tells us there are dark undercurrents, which these technologies have
not addressed.

Next, Schwab wants us to believe his rich friends have had nothing to do with the bad parts of our development, and in any case, there will be "disruptions" and new ways of doing things that will forever erase all of these problems.

However, to get to that bright future, we're going to have to make some changes, take off the guardrails, so to speak, loosen up some of the laws. But don't worry, he'll get some "private regulators" out there, discipline will be meted out by trade and professional organizations that won't let you pursue a living if you don't do what they want, and if at the end you still stand up and complain, well, he'll just get Big Tech to silence you.

Where did all these ideas come from?

We will investigate that in our next chapter.

*Chapter Three*

# Who's Responsible for This Garbage?

There's probably no better expert in the world to address the origins of the Fourth Industrial Revolution/Great Reset than Patrick Wood, an economist by training, author, and lecturer, who has studied the issue of globalization since the late 1970s.

Wood first became interested in the question of powerful groups of elites when, as a young financial analyst and writer, he noticed that upon his election in 1976, President Jimmy Carter picked a number of his advisors from a group called "the Trilateral Commission," founded in 1973 by David Rockefeller and Zbigniew Brzezinski (father of current MSNBC host, Mika Brzezinski).

In his 2016 book, *Technocracy Rising*, Wood recounts the Carter/Brzezinski relationship:

> President James Earl Carter, the Georgia peanut farmer turned politician who promised, "I will never lie to you," was chosen to join the Commission by Brzezinski in 1973. It was Brzezinski, in fact, who first identified Carter as presidential timber, and subsequently educated him in economics, foreign policy, and the ins-and-outs of world politics. Upon Carter's election, his first appointment placed Brzezinski as assistant to the president for national security matters. More commonly, he was called the

head of the National Security Council because he only answered
to the president; some rightly said Brzezinski held the second
most powerful position in the U.S.[1]

That's certainly not a bad position in which to find yourself, second
only in power to the president of the United States. Who wouldn't want
that gig, especially if it came without the need to do any campaigning?

But this didn't happen without decades of prior work. And it certainly began prior to the creation of the Trilateral Commission in 1973.
Woods identifies the roots of this globalist movement as beginning
with the French philosopher Auguste Comte (1798–1857), generally
credited as being the father of modern sociology and considered the
first philosopher of science. In the intellectual ferment of the day, it's
easy to understand how he came to believe that scientific knowledge
was the only authentic knowledge. This quickly gave rise to what's
called "scientism," professing that science alone is what can answer all
questions. For those who came to identify as "progressives," namely,
those who believe human society is evolving toward perfection, this
religion of technocrats (dubbed "Technocracy" by its creators) offered a
useful path toward the achievement of their utopian dreams. As Wood
explains:

> Industrialization was enabled by science, technology and inven-
> tion. As knowledge increased, it was surmised that society must
> change along with it, or at least adapt to it. Progressives called for
> bigger government run by qualified managers with diminishing
> personal liberty and national sovereignty, but they simultaneously
> fought to reduce waste and increase efficiency in government. The
> emphasis on efficiency drove many progressives into Technocracy
> since science appeared to be the only pathway to achieve it.[2]

It can then be seen how this new Technocracy might interact with
other such ideologies, such as progressivism, socialism, fascism, and

even capitalism. The scientists and engineers would then be in control of society, but without having to contend with the pesky problems of democracy and individual rights. (When I speak of democracy, my readers understand I'm not talking about a pure democracy, but our constitutional republic, a system of majority rule and minority rights, in which elected representatives are given authority to make decisions that they must defend at the next election if they wish to remain in office.)

Wood goes on to claim that many groups in history, such as the Nazis, fascists, and communists, would adopt many of these principles but were unwilling to allow the growth of a scientific elite leadership class who would oversee the society. These groups may have been evil, but they understood a challenge to their authority when they saw it.

Because of its open and democratic institutions, the West seemed to present the best opportunity for the creation of this scientific/engineering elite, or Technocracy. The people simply had to be persuaded to accept this gentle tyranny, which would, of course, free them from all their worries.

The colossal death toll of World War I, with more than nine million dead, should have presented an enormous opportunity for the development of a Technocratic State, but those brief dreams were dashed by the technological and social changes brought about by the war, which came to fruition with the Roaring Twenties.

During the early part of the twentieth century, the Technocracy flame was further developed and kept alive by people like Frederick Taylor, an American mechanical engineer best known for his work *The Principles of Scientific Management*, and Walter Rauthenstrauch, a professor at Columbia University.

Many of these ideas would be embraced by a group of intellectuals who broke away from Columbia to form what became known as the New School, led by two men, Thorstein Veblen and his young protégé, Howard Scott. In 1921, Veblen released his grand masterpiece, a book titled *Engineers and the Price System*, in which he wrote:

If the country's productive industry were competently organized as a systematic whole and were then managed by competent technicians with an eye to maximum production of goods and services instead of, as now, being manhandled by ignorant businessmen with an eye single to maximum profits; the resulting output of goods and services would doubtless exceed the current output by several hundred percent.[3]

It was only with the arrival of the Stock Market Crash of 1929 and the Great Depression in the United States that an opportunity arose for the Technocrats. As Wood recounts:

Society was ripe for Technocracy during the depths of the Great Depression. It certainly appeared that capitalism was dead. Joblessness, deflation, hunger, anger at politicians and capitalists, and other social stresses had people begging for an explanation as to what went wrong and what could be done to fix it. Technocracy, Inc. had both: Capitalism had died a natural death, and a Technocracy oriented society would save them. The engineers, scientists and technicians who would operate this Technocratic Utopia would eliminate all waste and corruption, people would only have to work 20 hours per week, and every person would have a job. Abundance would be everywhere![4]

The moment of the Technocrats had seemingly arrived. The carnage of millions dying in a World War was not enough, but surely the president of the United States, Franklin Roosevelt, could be talked into such a scheme!

Roosevelt did adopt some of their ideas, like suspending the gold standard, confiscating the gold of private citizens, and nationalizing certain industries, but he didn't want to hand power over to the technocrats. As Wood explains:

In any case, American democracy was found to be unwilling to entertain Technocracy, and it was soundly repudiated for all of these reasons:

- National sovereignty and the Constitutional form of government were not dispensable.
- Nobody was willing to give up private property or the possibility of accumulating private wealth.
- The apparent similarities between Technocracy, Inc. and Nazi fascism were abhorrent to most Americans.
- The grandiose promises of Technocracy were seen as so much "free lunch," and toward the end of the Great Depression, everybody knew from experience that there was no such thing.[5]

According to Wood, the Technocrats didn't get their way during the Great Depression, or World War II. However, in the aftermath of the defeat of Nazi Germany, some of their best scientists and engineers came to America by way of a CIA program called "Operation Paperclip," infiltrating our pharmaceutical, defense, and space industries, led most notably by former Nazi rocket scientist Werner Von Braun, widely credited for heading the American program to put a man on the moon.

The Technocrats didn't win the battle for public opinion, but even the Nazi Technocrats were able to find a home in American industry and government work.

The monster of Technocracy slumbered in the American nation, waiting for the opportunity to rise and seize power.

* * *

Patrick Wood was kind enough to give an interview to me, as he has now been lecturing about the dangers of the Technocracy for more than forty years. He's a tall, distinguished-looking man with a full head of white hair and closely cropped beard, usually dressed in a suit and tie, and reminds one of a distinguished college professor.

This should not come as much of a surprise, considering that his long-time collaborator in this research was Dr. Anthony Sutton, a former economics professor at Stanford University and member of the Hoover Institute for War, Peace, and Revolution. Sutton was jokingly referred to by his colleagues as the "Hoover vacuum cleaner," on account of his voracious appetite for details.[6]

Wood's interest in Technocracy began shortly after the 1976 Presidential Election of Jimmy Carter and his vice president, Walter Mondale.

> As a young financial analyst and writer, I carefully followed Carter's initial round of appointees to the top positions in his cabinet and other important posts. After all, Carter had made a big campaign pitch about being an "establishment outsider" with few contacts within the Beltway. Who would he bring to the table? As the list of appointees piled up, I noticed that several were members of the Trilateral Commission, whatever that was, and my curiosity was immediately peaked. After digging up and sifting through a list of Trilateral Commission members, and seeing over a dozen Trilateral Appointees, it became immediately obvious that some sort of coup was underway, but what?[7]

In our interview I began by asking him to explain the role played by Zbigniew Brzezinski, Carter's patron; Henry Kissinger, President Nixon's National Security adviser and secretary of state; as well as the contribution of David Rockefeller, who seemed to be the financial dynamo behind the modern-day origins of this Technocracy. I also asked about the Trilateral Commission, and its subsequent evolution into the World Economic Forum created by Klaus Schwab and his designation of the Fourth Industrial Revolution/Great Reset.

> Let's start with the Trilateral Commission, founded in 1973. That was the beginning of modern globalization. What happened in the years before 1973 was largely unsuccessful. And the global

elite knew that. So, they embarked on a new mission with the Trilateral Commission, to essentially do an end run around national sovereignty around the world.

And to create what they called "A New International Economic Order." That was their marching orders.

It was created by David Rockefeller, the chairman of Chase Manhattan Bank and from the Rockefeller oil dynasty. The other founder was a political scientist from Columbia University named Zbigniew Brzezinski. The two of them founded the Trilateral Commission.

The significance of Brzezinski being at Columbia University is that he was aware of what Technocracy was because that's where it was developed in the early 1930s. Brzezinski wrote a book called *Between Two Ages: America's Role in the Technetronic Era.* That book foretold the Technetronic era we're living in today.

That book endeared him to David Rockefeller, who was looking for a way to extend his monopoly power by capturing the resources of the world.[8]

The outlines of the story Patrick Wood told were clear, and easy to follow. This Technocracy ideal, a world run by engineers and scientists, was essentially developed in the late nineteenth century and found an academic home at Columbia University in the 1930s. The philosophy did not sway Franklin Roosevelt but did sway Adolf Hitler, who depended not on politicians, but scientists and engineers to run his Third Reich.

Brzezinski further developed these ideas in his book, which caught the attention of David Rockefeller. The Technocrats then saw an opportunity to rebrand their philosophy and, within a few short years, had captured the presidency with the election of Jimmy Carter and his new National Security Advisor, Zbigniew Brzezinski.

I think it's important to understand that Technocracy can't accurately be called communism or democracy. It is best understood as a monopoly on power, held jointly by Big Business and Big Government.

And in all honesty, while Big Government may hold the club, the real power lies with the financial strength of Big Business.

The robber barons of old, like the Rockefellers, weren't interested in a vibrant, free market. They didn't like unions, and their perfect world was the company town where the residents owned little and were dependent on the company for practically everything.

The robber barons were interested in a closed market, a monopoly, or what might look to the public like relatively few players, when in truth, the same group of powerful individuals controlled all the various entities.

Wood continued with his explanation of the formation of the Trilateral Commission, the role of President Jimmy Carter, the participation of the United Nations, and the rise of China as an experimental laboratory for this Technocratic ideal:

> The two of them [Rockefeller and Brzezinski] founded the Trilateral Commission, this "New International Economic Order," then immediately passed the baton to the United Nations. In 1974, the United Nations passed a resolution called "The Establishment of a New International Economic Order" with their language, and that's where it was introduced to the United Nations.
>
> From 1973 on, many things happened, specifically with China. In 1976, when Jimmy Carter was elected, and when Zbigniew Brzezinski became his National Security advisor, and both Carter and his vice-president [Walter Mondale] were members of the Trilateral Commission. Brzezinski is the one who is credited with bringing Deng Xiaoping to the United States to wine and dine him and bring him back into the global economic fold. This is widely acknowledged in textbooks, that Brzezinski was the brains behind the introduction of China to the world stage.
>
> Henry Kissinger also had a big hand in that. Kissinger was also a founding member of the Trilateral Commission.[9]

According to Wood, the members of the Trilateral Commission had sufficient contacts among the foreign policy elite that they could reasonably expect to be placed in the top positions in government, regardless of whether there was a Republican or Democratic administration in power. President Nixon, a Republican, had Henry Kissinger as his National Security advisor, and Democrat Jimmy Carter had Zbigniew Brzezinski as his National Security advisor and confidant.

The Technocrats finally reached the center of American power in the 1970s, after more than forty years of effort, and could begin putting their plans into action, starting with a test case for their ambitions.

Their choice?

Not the United States, where they knew they'd run into predictable opposition. Instead, the Technocrats chose China, as Wood explained:

> China looked like North Korea does today. They had no economic system, there was starvation, they had no industry, and it was a horrible, oppressive culture. However, it was a blank slate to do anything that the Rockefeller crowd wanted done. When Zbigniew Brzezinski got a hold of Deng Xiaoping, Brzezinski did not teach China about free market economics or capitalism. He taught them about Technocracy. That's one reason the ascendance of China has been so dramatic. They have excelled at using that, exploiting it, expanding it, and exporting it to the world. China is the poster child for Technocracy. They have perfected surveillance, artificial intelligence, the use of social credit scores to keep their citizens in line, and strong-arming the population, forcing them to do whatever they want. If they don't comply willingly, they just start shooting them. That is basically the story of China and how it came to be where it is today.[10]

Wood's presentation of the history was so succinct and provided me with such a different lens with which to view the rise of China, it was momentarily disorienting. Had such a close relationship existed between the Chinese communist party and the Technocrats since the

1970s? Was a significant part of our foreign policy establishment working with the Chinese communist party since the late 1970s?

However, a publicly available text of the first exchange between
Zbigniew Brzezinski and Deng Xiaoping on May 21, 1978, currently
exists on the website of the US-China Institute. It seems that Brzezinski
was so interested in normalizing the relationship with China that he
didn't mind selling out the people of Taiwan or concealing what he was
doing from the American public.

> **Brzezinski:** With respect to discussions about normalization,
> which we trust will begin in June, I would like to suggest that
> these discussions be kept confidential and that no advance public-
> ity be issued. I think continuing such discussions in the context of
> confidentiality would make their success more likely and would
> minimize some of the political complications which, at one point
> or another, will be inevitable in our own country. Although my
> visit here is not to negotiate normalization, I would like to think
> of it as contributing a step forward and not a step backward. We
> only want to go forward, and I hope you will interpret this visit
> in such a fashion.
>
> We start with the premise which we have already accepted
> before—that there is only one China, not one-and-a-half Chinas
> or two Chinas or China and Taiwan. For us there is only one
> China. We also believe that the three key points provide the
> framework for defining our basic relationship. There are certain
> basic difficulties that we ourselves have to overcome, but though
> these difficulties are for us to overcome precisely because there is a
> relationship between us you have to be aware of these difficulties
> and be sensitive to them.
>
> The fundamental difficulty is how will the American people
> understand the nature of this historically transitional period in
> our relations with the people of Taiwan following normalization.
> During that historically transitional period domestic difficulties
> in the U.S. would be far minimized if our hope and expectation

that the internal and purely domestic resolution of Chinese problems would be such that it would be peaceful and that our own hopes in this respect would not be specifically contradicted.[11]

One doesn't need to be a diplomat to understand when you're being betrayed. Brzezinski was clearly throwing Taiwan overboard in favor of China. And in return, Brzezinski seemed to be begging the Chinese not to do anything that would unduly alarm the wary American public. It seems both sides understood the bargain they were making. As one reads the account, it's difficult to escape the feeling that Brzezinski was acting like the diplomat of a subservient nation, while China was being treated as the dominant nation, perhaps even the victor in a great war.

Brzezinski remained a friend to the leaders of the Chinese communist party all his life and when he died in June 2017 was remembered fondly in the pages of *China Daily* in an opinion piece titled "Brzezinski and His Insightful Wisdom Will Be Missed." Here's a sample of what they wrote:

The passing of Zbigniew Brzezinski last week came as a shock because a little more than a month ago he was still making public appearances and commenting on the Korean Peninsula issue. In the past week, many of my Chinese journalist friends who had interviewed him or attended his lectures recalled on WeChat Moments their fond memories of the great strategist.

For many of us, Brzezinski was a man of wisdom with a great understanding of the world and China. As the U.S. national security advisor in the Jimmy Carter administration, Brzezinski played a key role in the normalization of diplomatic relations between the United States and the People's Republic of China in 1979 . . .

To my generation, Brzezinski was one of several wise US politicians known to Chinese. Others included former US Secretary of State Henry Kissinger and former US National Security Advisor Brent Scowcroft.[12]

When you're eulogized by the Chinese communist party, I question when you reach the Pearly Gates if you're going to get a good reception from Saint Peter. I don't think you're going to the good place with fluffy clouds and angels playing music.

More likely, you're going to spend eternity in a much warmer climate.

Wood continued with the history of how the Technocrats, once established in government, figured out how to remain in powerful positions:

> The early members of the Trilateral Commission told us repeatedly that they were not interested in a political takeover. And yet, during the Carter administration, Carter and Mondale were members, Brzezinski was a member, and at one point, every cabinet member Carter had, except for one, was a member of the Trilateral Commission. It looked like a clean sweep.
>
> Then, on the other hand, they say they're not interested in a political takeover. They just wanted to create a New International Economic Order.
>
> But what we found out was that America represented the policy generating strongman of global economics. And anybody who could get their hands on the engine of economics would be able to control the entire planet. And that's exactly what they did as time went onwards from 1976.[13]

The narrative of Patrick Wood conforms to the known facts about the early Trilateral Commission and China's entry into the global economic community. These were not low-level government employees. They were the top officials in our government, and they were enacting plans they'd never discussed among the American public.

However, they had to work slowly, as they did not have the support of the voters for many of these initiatives. They would need to be present in every presidential administration going forward. As Wood detailed the various administrations:

These technocrats have represented left and right, liberal and conservative, the political labels mean nothing to them. They operated through the Reagan administration, George H.W. Bush was a member of the Trilateral Commission, then you had Bill Clinton and Al Gore, both of whom were members of the Trilateral Commission. They brought into their government many members of the Trilateral Commission. Then with George W. Bush, you had Dick Cheney, who was a powerful member of the Trilateral Commission. Then you had Obama, who was completely surrounded in his intelligence community by members of the Trilateral Commission. Completely surrounded.

The same thing happened, maybe to a lesser extent in the Trump administration, and now you have the Biden administration.[14]

In the interview, Wood went on to tell a curious story about Henry Kissinger simply showing up at the White House and having at least two unscheduled meetings with President Trump. This is highly irregular, as meetings are supposed to be scheduled and on the daily agenda, and yet it testifies to Kissinger's continuing influence more than forty years after he left the White House, despite not being able to set foot in several countries around the world who have designated him a war criminal for his actions during the Vietnam War.

In what may or may not have been a coincidence, one of these times was right after Trump had fired FBI Director James Comey. As reported by Chris Cillizza of CNN:

The White House press pool was called into the Oval Office just before noon eastern time for what they expected to be a photo op between Trump and the Russian foreign minister Sergey Lavrov since the two men were scheduled to huddle earlier today.

But it wasn't Lavrov they found sitting with the president! It was Henry Kissinger, best known for his role as Secretary of State to President Nixon!

Reporters asked Trump about the firing of FBI Director James Comey. Trump responded, briefly, that Comey was simply "not doing a good job." It was apparently lost on Trump that the last 16 hours had been dominated by comparisons between Nixon's "Saturday Night Massacre"—where he jettisoned the independent counsel investigating Watergate—and Trump's decision to part ways with Comey.[15]

Cillizza of CNN claimed that Kissinger's unexpected appearance was just another example of the Trump circus, a whirlwind of incompetence, just a step or two away from disaster. And yet, given what was going on with Trump and the former FBI director, who had just been fired not twenty-four hours earlier, another interpretation, based on the decades of work by Patrick Wood, was plausible.

Trump was showing his independence by firing FBI Director Comey, and perhaps Kissinger went in to deliver a threat from the globalists. Kissinger may have thought it would be a secret meeting, but

Henry Kissinger and Donald Trump during Kissinger's unexpected visit to the White House. *(Official White House Photo by Shealah Craighead; accessed on Wikimedia) Commons)*

Trump turned the situation around by inviting the press in for a photo opportunity. Kissinger, well into his nineties, couldn't quickly scurry away but instead sat in his chair looking like nothing more than a shriveled little troll as the press arrived.

I defy you to look at that picture and come to any other conclusion.

Trump ended his term (maybe just the first?) as combative as when he entered, although he had not done much to harm the globalists or halt their march to a Technocratic state.

* * *

I asked Patrick Wood to explain how the Trilateral Commission fed into the World Economic Forum and the Great Reset, and as usual, he had a clear and concise answer:

> Back in the early days of the Trilateral Commission, they were very reticent to come out and speak about their plans. They did it every once in a while, but we beat them up so badly, they decided not to come out and play anymore. They were relatively secretive about their plans and operations. Even David Rockefeller, in his memoirs, admitted that they were very secretive about their meetings and plans.
>
> By comparison, the World Economic Forum is made up of the same type of people as the Trilateral Commission, but it has a much broader membership. You have the media, you have lawyers, politicians, and the CEOs of giant companies. It was the same kind of people you saw in the Trilateral Commission. It has a much broader membership, and a much larger one, but still the same mix of people as you saw in the Trilateral Commission.
>
> However, the World Economic Forum is completely open about their plans. They have an extensive website with tons and tons of articles that you could get lost in. In the articles they declare exactly what their plans are. It's also important to note that the World Economic Forum is so tightly wedded to the

United Nations that it can be hard to see where the two groups differ at all.[16]

Woods describes the path trod by many revolutionary groups, from the communists of Russia and China, to the fascists of Italy, to the Nazis of Germany. If you know the public isn't going to support your message, you lie about your ultimate plans. You convince the good people to surrender or stay silent as you implement your plans.

I asked Wood if it was accurate to say that Klaus Schwab and the World Economic Forum were using issues such as "sustainable development," "climate change," and "racism and gender issues" as a way to divide people, making them more vulnerable to the plans of the globalists. He agreed it was a tactic they used but said it was also a strategy to keep people from looking too closely at their plans:

> The World Economic Forum is to complete the plans of the New International Economic Order and the Trilateral Commission. That's what the Great Reset is all about. It's been forty-five, fifty years in the making. The Great Reset is the New International Economic Order. This is Technocracy warmed over from the 1930s. It's a resource-based system where they will control all the resources and you and I will own nothing. In fact, Klaus Schwab even says that. You can look it up.[17]

Sometimes your understanding of an issue depends on when you enter the conversation. If you had entered the conversation within the last ten years, you might think this all began with Klaus Schwab, the World Economic Forum, and the Fourth Industrial Revolution. However, you'd be sorely mistaken. If you just focused on the work of the Trilateral Commission, you look to Henry Kissinger, David Rockefeller, Zbigniew Brzezinski, and the early 1970s. However, you'd fail to see the links going back to the 1930s and Columbia University. That's why it's often so enlightening to talk to an expert like Patrick

Wood. An expert can give a deep historical perspective of an issue that you wouldn't otherwise understand.

Probably one of the most surprising parts of my interview with Patrick Wood was when he talked about how oblivious many of the early members of the Trilateral Commission were to the unpopularity of their ideas among the public. Wood recalls:

> There was a paternalistic attitude by members of the Trilateral Commission regarding the rest of the world. They figured since they were the bright ones, the ones with PhDs and that sort of stuff, that they had a leg up on everybody else in deciding what was good and what was bad. We repeatedly ran into this attitude where what they'd say is something like, "Well, what we're doing is for everybody's good. It's for the global good. So, why would anybody take exception to it?"
>
> We took exception to it, and we told them that. But they just couldn't understand why we'd be upset about their plans to help the world. It was just crazy. I still shake my head.
>
> This is really the heartbeat of what I call "scientism." Scientism sets up science as a god. It's kind of an extension of humanism in a way. It sets up science as a god that can do no wrong. And they reject any other type of moral, ethical, or Biblical restraint. It doesn't matter. All of this is just nonsense to them.
>
> And they believe the god of science is the only path to finding out about the nature of man and the universe. This allows them to come up with some very strange ideas about their way being the only sensible way. And everybody else, with a different idea, is a crackpot.[18]

I found Patrick Wood's comments to be extremely helpful in explaining the mindset of these globalists/Technocrats. They genuinely believed what they were saying. They think the rest of us are idiots in need of being saved by them. They reject all other sources of morality, be it religious, ethical, or moral. It is accurate to call them materialists, and yet even the most ardent materialist can still live an ethical life if they respect the rights of others just as much as they respect these rights for themselves.

In some ways it's quite sad, as one might say these globalists suffer from a "God-shaped hole" in their soul, where God used to be, and are desperately trying to fill this void with the god of scientism. They do not engage with the moral and spiritual complexities of life and thus most closely resemble a general who conducts a battle far from the front, forever blind to what's happening at the tip of the spear, where success or failure is determined. They live an antiseptic life, devoid of joy or suffering, and pass from this world with little or no spiritual development.

The next subject I covered in my conversation with Wood was my frustration with something I couldn't find in the writings of Klaus Schwab or the globalists. Their writings spoke abundantly of "communication, collaboration, and a common set of values" but contained little information about what happened to those who, after a period of "communication," simply didn't agree to their "common set of values." I asked if Wood could point me to any sources that explained how these globalists planned to deal with dissenters. This was his response:

> We can certainly see the anecdotal evidence for that with all the people who've been canceled, kicked out, thrown out, shamed, and in some cases, probably murdered. The pattern has been very clear. Anybody who does not agree with their narrative is in jeopardy of being removed from the scene.
>
> It's kind of what China does. In China, they call it "disappearing" people. They haven't gone quite that far in the West to specifically kill somebody. But "disappearing" people is the name of the game. We see this in the medical community. For example, the Great Barrington Declaration [opposing the COVID-19 lockdowns, masking regulations, and vaccine mandates] had a couple hundred thousand signatures, with about three thousand being

top scientists and medical professionals. Every one of those people was canceled by the censorship culture.

And that wasn't by mistake. It was an intentional campaign to crush anybody who had an alternative narrative to COVID-19. And we see this all over the major media, social media, and with many large corporations who are censoring people they don't like for one reason or another.[19]

I found it difficult to disagree with anything that Wood was claiming. Anybody paying attention to the media understands that, in the past several years, especially since the appearance of COVID-19, there has been nothing less than an assault on free speech. The old answer to the question of speech that people believe to be wrong is more speech to counter what is believed to be false.

The answer to bad speech is good speech and trusting people to be able to tell the difference.

This principle no longer seems to be part of the operating system of our civilization.

Instead, the motives of the speaker were attacked, usually with some of the most heinous allegations possible today, and that person was removed from the discussion on the grounds that many found the comments objectionable, or that such speech created a significant risk of public harm. If we lose free speech, we lose our ability to think and can only blindly follow the dictates of those who believe they have our best interests at heart.

One of the final questions I wanted Patrick Wood to address was something that has long bothered me. Because of our tradition of free speech in the West, as well as individual autonomy, we have a different operating system than an individual in China or Russia, which have a long history of cowering under the dictates of the latest authoritarian ruler. Although there have been suspicious deaths of dissidents in the West, I'd agree that little hard evidence has been presented to establish this as a pattern utilized by the powerful in our society.

I asked Patrick whether he agreed that in the West it would be difficult to force these changes upon us. But, if they could somehow get people to acquiesce to their plans, or remain silent, that it would greatly increase their chances of success.

In other words, they could not succeed by force.

However, they could succeed by subterfuge or somehow obtaining our consent, such as the old superstition about how a vampire could not enter a house without the invitation of the homeowner. We needed to invite, or at least acquiesce to, the entry of the vampire of globalism into our house. Wood detailed a specific change to the strategy of the globalists that came about around 1974:

> Richard Gardner, a founding member of the Trilateral Commission, and a professor, wrote an article in 1974 in *Foreign Affairs* magazine, with the title "The Hard Road to World Order." You can find it on the internet; it's been scanned. What he said, and this is a direct quote, was, "It will look like a great booming, buzzing confusion, but an end run around national sovereignty, eroding it piece by piece, will accomplish much more than the old-fashioned frontal assault."
>
> The game changed in 1973 with the formation of the Trilateral Commission. Prior to that you had the old-fashioned frontal assault. Then Gardner was saying there needed to be an end-run around national sovereignty. And that's exactly what they've done for the past forty-five or fifty years, chipping away, death by a thousand cuts, piece by piece, eroding national sovereignty.
>
> Probably the best example today is the European Union [EU]. The EU has taken over virtually every single function of the countries that it presides over. You can say on one hand, there's still a national government in Spain, Switzerland, and Germany. Yes, there is. But do they have the same power today that they had, say, thirty years ago? No, of course they don't.
>
> The EU is now making all of the significant policy decisions for Europe for those individual countries. This has been the

standard operating procedure for Technocracy, to chip away at national sovereignty and eventually remove the political structure altogether. That's been a goal since the 1930s.[20]

If one looks at the globalists like any other revolutionary movement, it becomes easy to understand their tactics. A frontal assault on the institutions of government was not likely to lead to success. Instead, it was important for them to work incrementally. The globalists are nothing if not patient.

As we wrapped up our interview, Wood suggested three things to me. First, he suggested I reread *Brave New World*, written by Aldous Huxley in 1933, the same year Technocracy established itself at Columbia University. "In *Brave New World*, there's no political structure," said Wood. "The world is run by the scientists and engineers. The book was a direct attack on Technocracy, so I suggest you reread it to see what things have come to pass, and what might be ahead."

Second, he suggested I simply go to the website for the World Economic Forum and read their papers. "It's all out in the open," he said.

Third, he suggested I read the work of Israeli academic Yuval Hariri, probably the most important adviser to Klaus Schwab: "If you want to understand Klaus Schwab, you need to understand Yuval Hariri. He's got some pretty strange ideas. He's all about transhumanism and the singularity. His latest book is called *Homo Deus*, which means man is now God. Gives you a good idea of the man's humility."

I promised to do all of those things but first had some other questions. I wanted to know more about David Rockefeller's book where he discussed the early Trilateral Commission and the book *Between Two Ages*, which first brought Columbia University Professor Zbigniew Brzezinski to the attention of the aged billionaire.

\* \* \*

In 2002, when he was eighty-seven years old, David Rockefeller published his 517-page autobiography, *Memoirs*. Chapter 27 is titled "Proud Internationalist" and details some of his pursuits in that area. After opening with a day in his life (October 23, 1995), in which he met various friends at the fiftieth anniversary of the United Nations, including Fidel Castro, Rockefeller then turned to his critics:

> For more than a century ideological extremists at either end of the political spectrum have seized upon well-publicized incidents such as my encounter with Castro to attack the Rockefeller family for the inordinate influence they claim we wield over American political and economic institutions. Some even believe we are part of a secret cabal working against the best interests of the United States, characterizing my family and me as "internationalists" and of conspiring with others around the world to build a more integrated global political and economic structure—one world, if you will. If that's the charge, I stand guilty, and I am proud of it.[21]

It's a bold paragraph, which does several things. First, he paints himself as a centrist, by claiming that he's attacked by "ideological extremists at either end of the political spectrum." He mentions the claims of those who assert he's part of a group of internationalists. And instead of denying these claims, he proudly confesses to being a supporter of an "integrated global political and economic structure—one world, if you will." It's a disarming approach.

And yet, he also engages in the demonization of his enemies. While you may believe the "populist" label is a new insult wielded by the left, it's a little surprising to read the vitriol with which Rockefeller uses the populist label against his enemies on the right or left, in 2002:

> The anti-Rockefeller focus of these otherwise incompatible political positions owes much to Populism. "Populists" believe in conspiracies, and one of the most enduring is that a secret group of international bankers and capitalists and their minions, control

the world's economy. Because of my name and prominence as the head of Chase for many years, I have earned the distinction of "conspirator in chief" from some of these people.[22]

Let's imagine we put David Rockefeller in the witness chair of a courtroom and cross-examine him. He's the head of one of the largest banks in the world and criticizes his critics of the left and right, who question how Rockefeller and his fellow rich people are manipulating the world's economy. If we weren't dazzled by Rockefeller's wealth, would we accept him as a credible person to discount the claim that wealthy bankers were controlling a lot of the world? No, we would not.

Rockefeller used much the same approach of lightheartedly dismissing his critics when he discussed the establishment of the Trilateral Commission. Rockefeller wrote:

> No organization with which I have played a founding role has attracted as much public scrutiny and attention as the Trilateral Commission. Pat Robertson has insisted that Trilateral is trying to create a world government and claims that it springs "from the depths of something evil." My son Richard, when he was a student at Harvard in the 1970s, told me his friends assumed that Trilateral was part of a nefarious conspiracy.[23]

If we have a little different take on what Rockefeller is saying, he admits that presumably some of the smartest students in the country, those at Harvard University, didn't trust the Trilateral Commission. But Rockefeller did provide information about the founding of the Trilateral Commission and admits it was his idea:

> The idea for an organization including representatives from North America, Europe, and Japan—the three centers of democratic capitalism—resulted from my realization in the early 1970s that power relationships in the world had fundamentally changed. The United States, although still dominant, had declined relatively in

terms of its economic power as both Western Europe and Japan recovered from the devastation of World War II and entered a period of dramatic economic growth and expansion. As a result, the comity that characterized relationships among these regions for more than two decades had deteriorated alarmingly, and I believed something needed to be done.[24]

When it comes from Rockefeller's own pen, it's easy to understand why some populists might call him the "conspirator in chief." In his mind, he was certainly the founder. However, if one is to believe Rockefeller's account of what happened next, it's as if his simple charitable plan caused him to be accidentally swept up into the winds of history:

We cast our nets widely in terms of membership and recruited labor union leaders, corporate CEOs, prominent Democrats and Republicans, as well as distinguished academics, university presidents, and the heads of non-profits involved overseas. We assembled what we believed were the best minds in America. The Europeans and Japanese assembled delegations of comparable distinction.[25]

How could anybody possibly object to one of the world's richest men bringing together the most powerful and influential people of America, Western Europe, and Japan in the early 1970s? Of course, the rich and powerful always have such get-togethers because they want to do enormous good for the common people. The very idea that such get-togethers might be to retain or increase their power in an increasingly democratic world, well, it should be banned from all media!

And it was certainly a complete coincidence that among that first group of American politicians invited onto the Trilateral Commission was one who would go on to grab the ultimate prize:

The inclusion among that first group of an obscure Democratic governor of Georgia—James Earl Carter—had an unintended

consequence. A week after Trilateral's first executive committee meeting in Washington in December 1975, Governor Carter
announced that he would seek the Democratic nomination for
president of the United States. I have to confess that at the time
I thought he had little chance of success. Much to my amaze-
ment, however, he not only won the Democratic nomination but
defeated President Gerald Ford in the November election.[26]

Now, even though James Earl Carter was "an obscure Democratic
governor of Georgia," what might have made him such an attractive
recruit for the Trilateral Commission? Could it have been that he was
trained in the Navy as a nuclear engineer, making him an ideal aco-
lyte for this new religion of scientism in which engineers and scientists
would be the new high priests? The parade of good news for the members of the newly formed Trilateral Commission just kept coming in.
As Rockefeller recounted:

> Carter's campaign was subtly anti-Washington and antiestablish-
> ment, and he pledged to bring both new faces and new ideas into
> government. There was a good deal of surprise, then, when he
> chose fifteen members of Trilateral, many of whom had served in
> previous administrations, for his team, including Vice President
> Walter Mondale, Secretary of State Cyrus Vance, Secretary
> of Defense Harold Brown, Secretary of the Treasury Michael
> Blumenthal, and Zbigniew Brzezinski as national security advi-
> sor. In his 1975 autobiography, *Why Not the Best?*, Carter wrote
> that "membership on this commission has provided me with a
> splendid learning opportunity, and many of the other members
> have helped me in the study of foreign affairs."[27]

That must have set some all-time political record from starting your
organization in 1973 to winning the presidency in 1976 and stocking
the cabinet with fellow members. And while some who know their history will no doubt recollect that Carter quickly became bogged down

in various problems, such as the Iranian hostage crisis, runaway inflation, and gas shortages, even a new president from the opposing party
couldn't seem to break free of the Trilateral Commission. Rockefeller
wrote:

> In the 1980 presidential primary campaign, for instance, one of
> Ronald Reagan's supporters ran an advertisement that stated,
> "The people who brought you Jimmy Carter now want you to
> vote for George Bush," and highlighted the membership of both
> in Trilateral. I am not sure how many votes were changed by this
> ad, but such is the nature of politics in a democratic society. I
> should note, however, that President Reagan ultimately came to
> understand Trilateral's value and invited the entire membership
> to a reception at the White House in April 1984.[28]

When I read that paragraph, it only brings a sense of sadness to me,
seeming to show that Reagan also had to eventually knuckle under to
the power of the globalists. Maybe he just wanted to keep his enemies
close. Maybe it was simply about retaining power, the common flaw of
most political leaders.

I will give the final word to David Rockefeller, from the end of his
chapter "Proud Internationalist":

> These organizations reflect my belief in the principle of "construc-
> tive engagement." As an intelligence officer during World War II,
> I learned that my effectiveness depended on my ability to develop
> a network of people with reliable information and influence.
>
> Some may feel this technique is cynical and manipulative. I
> disagree. Such an approach enabled me to meet people who were
> useful in advancing goals and gave me opportunities to form last-
> ing friendships that have greatly enriched my life.[29]

I will leave it to you to decide whether that passage comforts you in the belief that the wealthy and powerful are looking out for your best interests, or whether that passage fills you with stark, raving terror.

* * *

Rockefeller provided the financial muscle for the Trilateral Commission, but the intellectual firepower came from former Columbia University Professor Zbigniew Brzezinski and his 1970 book *Between Two Ages: America's Role in the Technetronic Era*. There were only nineteen used copies of the original hardcover version available on Amazon, so I spent $49.50 to purchase one of the few remaining copies. Patrick Wood had given me good advice when he said I should get a copy, as it opened a clear window into the globalist mindset.

Like Schwab after him, Brzezinski spent much of the first portion of the book reciting history and the rapid pace of change. There's a technique that persuaders will engage in to gain your acceptance. They begin by telling you things with which you already agree and, once trust has been established, ever so gently try to lead you to their position. This is how Brzezinski opened his book:

> The paradox of our time is that humanity is becoming simultaneously more unified and more fragmented. That is the principle thrust of contemporary change. Time and space have become so compressed that global politics manifest a tendency toward larger, more interwoven forms of cooperation as well as toward the dissolution of established institutional and ideological loyalties. Humanity is becoming more integral and intimate even as the differences in the conditions of the separate societies are widening. Under these circumstances, proximity, instead of promoting unity, give rise to tensions prompted by a new sense of global congestion.[30]

As the opening of a book by a Columbia University professor, it's not bad. It's a little wonky but sets up a duality for you between unity and division. We feel excited, and at the same time we feel anxious. Pretty much how most people feel most of the time.

However, it's only when Brzezinski reaches "Part IV: The American Transition" (about two hundred pages in) that he starts to lay the groundwork for his new revolution. He characterizes our war with England as the first American Revolution, the Civil War as the Second American Revolution, and the time period after World War II as the Third American Revolution. And Brzezinski starts to engage in the same kind of breathless, gee-whiz, "ain't technology great" hyperbole that Klaus Schwab will use decades later:

> The third American revolution is even harder to define, for we are now in the middle of it and thus cannot be certain of its outcome. In one respect, however, it is easier to identify than the second, for its impact and its effect are more concentrated in time. The third revolution began gathering momentum after World War II, with the massive explosion in higher learning and the growing acceptance of the social primacy of education; with the union of national power and modern science crowned by the harnessing of nuclear energy and the federal government emerging as a major sponsor of scientific investigation; with the sudden birth of rapid continental communications, ranging from the world's most modern and developed highway systems, through rapid air passenger transport, to a uniquely effective instant transcontinental telephone system, and finally a nationwide television intimacy; with the transformation in managerial techniques wrought by the appearance of computers and other electronic devices that conquer complexity, distance, and even the diffusion of authority; and with the fading of industry as the most important source of employment for Americans.[31]

Can you believe that entire chunk of text contains only three sentences? A good rule of thumb is that when people use large, elaborate sentences, they want to overwhelm you.

Let me break down Brzezinski's argument.

More people are going to college; we need a new political system!

Big government funds big science; we need a new political system!

We have nuclear energy; we need a new political system!

We have telephones; we need a new political system!

We have highways; we need a new political system!

We have television; we need a new political system!

We have computers; we need a new political system!

One might just as easily have said: we have more flavors than just chocolate and vanilla ice cream, so we need a new political system!

As always, these avatars of change can't help but eventually tell you who they love, and who they wish would simply go away:

> In the process, it is creating three Americas in one. There is the emerging new America symbolized by the new complexes of learning, research, and development that link institutions of higher learning with society and create unprecedented opportunities for innovation and experimentation, in addition to sparking increased interest in the fine arts and culture, as is evidenced by new museums and art centers. Technetronic America is in the electronics laboratories and centers of learning along Route 128 surrounding Boston, it is in the academic-scientific conglomerates around Los Angeles and San Francisco; and it is in the new frontier industries. The suburban middle class increasingly gravitates toward this America, though frequently resenting its scientism and nostalgically yearning for more community and stability.[32]

In the next few paragraphs, Brzezinski discusses the other two Americas, the factory workers and "the first America, the pre-industrial America of sharecroppers and migrant workers from the Mississippi delta and of obsolescent miners from Appalachia, whose income has fallen behind the American average."[33]

It's clear from what follows that Brzezinski doesn't like factory workers or people who live in rural areas. His people of choice are those who worship institutions of "higher learning," have an appreciation for the "fine arts and culture," and long to be part of some "academic-scientific conglomerate," preferably around the cities of San Francisco, Los Angeles, or Boston.

However, it would be a mistake to associate Brzezinski with the radical socialist left, which would like to take more control over the resources. Brzezinski doesn't trust the government but apparently trusts the rich people, specifically the Technocrats:

> The government as an expression of the national will increasingly tends to be seen as unable to direct and coordinate national change effectively. It appears to neither articulate national goals nor to develop a sense of national direction. This feeling of uncertainty about national purpose is also magnified by the fading of the established political elite that has guided the nation since World War II. Primarily composed of men coming from the Eastern seaboard and connected with legal, corporate, and high financial circles, the political elite provided a sense of continuity within the framework of a pragmatic liberal consensus on the nature and character of modern industrial society.[34]

Brzezinski is genuinely telling the public that the problem is rich, powerful men from the Eastern seaboard. However, his later answer would be to replace them with people like Henry Kissinger, David Rockefeller, Zbigniew Brzezinski, and George H.W. Bush, all rich, powerful men from the Eastern seaboard!

And since we live in a democracy, where the use of raw power is generally frowned upon by the population, Brzezinski is clear about how the media must be used by the globalists:

The courtship of the press and the mass media is a necessary con-
comitant of courting the masses, since the masses are influenced
not only by direct appeal but also through the intermediary of
an "image," which is in part built up by the media themselves.
The desirability of this image puts a premium on advocating the
immediately popular and the fashionable rather than on formu-
lating broader objectives by focusing attention on basic philosophical questions concerning the meaning of a modern society.[35]

The globalists are telling us directly how much they need to use the
media to influence the public. It's even better if you can attach your
persuasion to some type of "image." Therefore, it's not that we disagree
about whether vaccines are being safely monitored, but that those who
think there are some safety concerns being overlooked are "anti-sci-
ence." If you disagree about some governmental program, then that
must mean you are a "right-wing terrorist."

Brzezinski seems to suggest how their plan would unfold:

More directly linked to the impact of technology, it involves the
gradual appearance of a more controlled and directed society.
Such a society would be dominated by an elite whose claim to
political power would rest on allegedly superior scientific know-
how. Unhindered by the restraints of traditional liberal values,
this elite would not hesitate to achieve its political ends by using
the latest modern techniques for influencing public behavior and
keeping society under close surveillance and control.[36]

I have to note that these globalists don't understand that they can't
really seem to convince the public and need to use "techniques for
influencing public behavior and keeping society under close surveillance and control." With these people it's always about controlling others. It's like a pathological state, the equivalent of a religious fanatic
always believing the end of the world is just around the corner:

Technological developments make it certain that modern society will require more and more planning. Deliberate management of the American future will become widespread, with the planner eventually displacing the lawyer as the key social legislator and manipulator. This will put a greater emphasis on defining goals and, by the same token, on a more self-conscious preoccupation with social ends.[37]

Brzezinski wants the engineer and the scientist to displace the attorney and the judge. What do you mean we need the courts and elections? We have science and social ends! And if the message isn't completely clear to you, Brzezinski will tie up all the loose ends at the end of his book:

To sum up: Though the objective of shaping a community of the developed nations is less ambitious than the goal of world government, it is more attainable. It is more ambitious than the concept of an Atlantic community but historically more relevant to the new spatial revolution. Though cognizant of present divisions between communist and non-communist nations, it attempts to create a new framework for international affairs not by exploiting these divisions but rather by striving to preserve and create openings for eventual reconciliation.[38]

Brzezinski seems to be REALLY disappointed he can't get his world government as quickly as he wanted. Still, he doesn't want you to be sad. It will still be bigger than that other Atlantic community. I think he's talking about NATO (North Atlantic Treaty Organization). What other large Atlantic organization existed in 1970? And he takes great pains so that the communists don't feel left out.

Brzezinski wants the communists to know there will be an eventual "reconciliation" between the communist and non-communist nations when they are absorbed by the globalists. In the view of the globalists, their model is the best of both words, efficient capitalism with zero political freedom.

They will buy your soul and your silence with their technological marvels. It's like we've gone back to the days of Mussolini and Hitler, who will at least make the trains run on time. Everything old is new again!

What could possibly go wrong with their plan to disenfranchise the rest of us without PhDs?

\* \* \*

One of the people who was not taken with the globalists of the Trilateral Commission in the 1970s was United States Senator Barry Goldwater, who famously ran against President Lyndon Johnson in 1964 for the presidency and lost in a landslide.

However, time has not been kind to Johnson, who is now almost universally believed by historians to have been a crooked politician[39] and a liar of immense proportions about our progress in the Vietnam War.[40] By contrast, the historic judgment of Senator Barry Goldwater has only risen with the passage of time, with even his political opponents acknowledging the man's honesty and integrity.[41] As Goldwater wrote in his 1979 memoirs:

> In my view, the Trilateral Commission represents a skillful, coordinated effort to seize control and consolidate the four centers of power—political, monetary, intellectual, and ecclesiastical. All this is to be done in the interests of creating a more peaceful, more productive world community. Throughout my public life and in these pages, I have refrained from judging other men's motives. I have no such hesitancy about judging their wisdom and the results of the actions taken.[42]

Goldwater saw the Trilateralists as an existential threat to the division of power in the United States, which had kept us free for more than two hundred years. He was especially concerned about a report presented at the plenary meeting of the Trilateral Commission on May 30–31, 1975, in Kyoto, Japan, which detailed their plans for a centralized economy, centralized political control through Congress, and a program to lower the job expectations of college graduates. In other words, increased misery for everyone. Goldwater was also concerned that:

> The report also suggested it would be helpful to impose prior restrictions on the press and restructure the laws of libel to check the power of the press. It seems to me I've suffered as greatly from an abusive press as any man in public life, but I get an itchy, uncomfortable feeling at the base of my spine when somebody suggests that government should control the news.[43]

Goldwater was attacked in the media as savagely as anybody of his time. However, he understood the importance of a free press, even when it wasn't fair. The system has the ability to correct itself, and the reversal of opinion about Goldwater and Johnson bears witness to this fact. But Goldwater wasn't done with his criticisms:

> The entire Trilateral approach is strictly economic. No recognition is given to the political condition. Total reliance is placed on materialism. The Commission emphasizes the necessity of eliminating artificial barriers to world commerce—tariffs, export duties, quotas—an objective I strongly support. What it proposes to substitute is an international economy managed and controlled by international monetary groups through the mechanism of international conglomerate manufacturing and business enterprise.[44]

One can clearly appreciate the cleverness of the globalists. Many conservatives would applaud the taking down of trade barriers, and yet the catch is what would replace them. At its heart, the difference between the globalists and the conservatives is about freedom. Do we trust the "hidden hand" of the open marketplace, or do we think the "smart people" need to pick winners and losers? Goldwater concludes by telling us how we would be treated by the globalists of the Trilateral Commission and their heirs:

> Populations are treated as nothing more than producing and consuming units. No attempt has been made to explain why the people of the Western world enjoy economic abundance. Freedom— spiritual, political, economic—is denied any importance in the Trilateral construction of the next century.[45]

We are currently more than forty years removed from Goldwater's warning, and yet it seems as if he could've written these words just yesterday. Freedom is under assault in ways that were unimaginable just a few short years ago. This is not an accident. It is part of a long-established plan.

This has nothing to do with social good, helping the children, or saving the whales.

It is a battle for control of everyone's future, and it is critically important we understand the enemy who lurks in the shadows.

## Chapter Four

# Then Came COVID-19

The more I study the globalists, the more I conclude they act a lot like that annoying used car salesman who will say anything to keep you from getting off the lot without making a purchase.

It's World War I; we need globalism.

It's the Great Depression; we need globalism.

It's World War II; we need globalism.

It's the Cold War; we need globalism.

It's the 1970s and with the World War II order breaking down; we need globalism.

It's 2001 and there's a War on Terror; we need globalism.

It's 2016 and technology is changing things; we need globalism.

It's 2020 and there's COVID-19; we need globalism.

However, before I get to the response of Klaus Schwab and the World Economic Forum, I need to get a few things out of the way.

It's my personal belief that the mainstream narrative of SARS-CoV-2 and COVID-19 is filled with so many lies it's difficult to detail all of them. Let me simply go over a few of the things I believe.

I think COVID-19 was a planned attack on civilization by the globalists, and they clearly broadcasted this by their exercise called Event 201. The website of the Center for Health Security described the gathering:

The Johns Hopkins Center for Health Security, in partnership
with the World Economic Forum and the Bill and Melinda Gates
Foundation hosted Event 201, a high-level pandemic exercise on
October 18, 2019, in New York, NY. The exercise illustrated areas
where public/private partnerships will be necessary during the
response to a severe pandemic in order to diminish large-scale
economic and societal consequences.[1]

I'd like you to recall that, from my perspective, whenever I hear
the expression "public-private partnership," I immediately translate
that into the word "fascism." I'm not saying you have to accept my
translation.

Just take my translation for a test spin and see how much it explains
about what happened next.

One of the big topics of discussion by the participants of Event
201 was how to deal with the spread of misinformation and strate-
gies to combat free speech. There were discussions of lockdowns and
the rapid development of new vaccines, rather than therapeutics that
would quickly knock down the severe consequences of this new viral
infection.

Striking, isn't it, when you consider how the ensuing months of
2020 unfolded?

But let's assume for a moment that SARS-CoV-2 wasn't an intentional act, but rather a negligent one. Scientists were playing around
with bat viruses, figuring they might someday cause a problem in
humans, and one of their creations escaped from the lab.

Would they take responsibility?

Hell, no! They'd lie their asses off about it.

The only problem was that in 2016, in an article in *Nature*, they'd
triumphantly told the world they'd been able to make these bat corona-
viruses able to infect humans. The title of the article was "Engineered
Bat Virus Stirs Debate Over Risky Research." Let's read a few paragraphs, shall we?

An experiment that created a hybrid version of a bat coronavirus—one related to the virus that causes SARS (severe acute respiratory syndrome)—has triggered renewed debate over whether engineering lab variants of viruses with possible pandemic potential is worth the risks.

In an article published in *Nature Medicine* on 9 November, scientists investigated a virus called SHC014, which is found in horseshoe bats in China. The researchers created a chimeric virus, made up of surface proteins of SHC014 and the backbone of a SARS virus that had been adapted to grow in mice and to mimic human disease. The chimera infected human airway cells—proving that the surface protein of SHC014 has the necessary structure to bind to a key receptor on the cells and to infect them. It also caused disease in mice, but did not kill them.[2]

There you have, if not a smoking gun, at least a significant amount of smoke. Scientists were attempting to graft the surface proteins of a virus from horseshoe bats, SHC014, and the "backbone of a SARS virus" and succeeded. The virus was then able to infect human airway cells. However, this generated some significant concerns among scientists:

> But other virologists question whether this information gleaned from the experiment justifies the potential risk. Although the extent of any risk is difficult to assess, Simon Wain-Hobson, a virologist at the Pasteur Institute in Paris, points out that the researchers have created a virus that "grows remarkably well" in human cells. "If this virus escaped, nobody could predict the trajectory," he says.
>
> This argument is essentially a rerun of the debate over whether to allow lab research that increases the virulence, ease of spread or host range of dangerous pathogens —what is known as "gain of function" research. In October 2014, the US government

imposed a moratorium on federal funding of such research on the viruses that cause SARS, influenza and MERS (Middle East Respiratory Syndrome, a deadly disease caused by a virus that sporadically jumps from camels to people).[3]

To put it plainly, the scientists who were working in this field were so terrified of their viruses engineered under "gain of function" research escaping the lab that they issued a moratorium in October 2014 on this research.

And did our lead public health official on COVID-19, Dr. Anthony Fauci, "follow the science" regarding the likely origin of the virus, as he repeatedly told Americans to do? The evidence suggests he did not. From the *New York Post* on June 2, 2021:

> Dr. Anthony Fauci was warned that the coronavirus had possibly been "engineered" and appeared to be taking reports about it seriously—at the same time he was publicly downplaying the notion of the virus being created in a lab, according to his emails.
>
> Meanwhile, Fauci, America's top expert in infectious diseases, also got a "personal thank you" for backing the "natural origin" theory from the head of a nonprofit that used a $3.4 million government grant to fund research at the Chinese lab suspected of creating the virus, the emails show.[4]

Is it a coincidence that Dr. Anthony Fauci, our country's top infectious disease specialist, lied about the possible origins of this virus and that the most powerful organizations in the world, including Johns Hopkins University, Klaus Schwab's World Economic Forum, and the Bill and Melinda Gates Foundation worked together on Event 201, which envisioned just such a scenario?

Possibly, but let's say I haven't quite proved my claim to your satisfaction.

Let's go further down the list of "mistakes" made by Dr. Fauci.

Next, there's the question of how to respond to the virus. And again, Dr. Fauci seems pretty determined not to engage in a scientific give-and-take, but to act in ways more befitting an authoritarian regime of scientists.

The first rule of an authoritarian is to silence the opposition, which it appears Fauci and the head of the National Institutes of Health, Dr. Francis Collins, did. In fact, the allegations against these two men were so egregious that the Editorial Board of the *Wall Street Journal* felt compelled to write an opinion piece about the issue on December 21, 2021:

> In public, Anthony Fauci and Francis Collins urged Americans to "follow the science." In private, the two sainted public-health officials schemed to quash dissenting views from top scientists. That's the troubling but fair conclusion from emails obtained recently via the Freedom of Information Act by the American Institute for Economic Research.
>
> The tale unfolded in October 2020 after the launch of the Great Barrington Declaration, a statement by Harvard's Martin Kulldorff, Oxford's Sunetra Gupta and Stanford's Jay Bhattacharya against blanket pandemic lockdowns. They favored a policy of what they called "focused protection" of high-risk populations such as the elderly or those with medical conditions. Thousands of scientists signed the declarations—if they were able to learn about it.[5]

There's the setup that any good globalist would be salivating over. Anthony Fauci and Francis Collins sit atop the public health pyramid of America, distributing billions of federal dollars to their favorite researchers and projects. In the mind of the typical globalist, this is a recipe for success.

But even in science, the democratic, free-thinking urges prevail. Not all the top people in science will go along with the consensus. In fact, the best scientists are usually those who ruthlessly question the prevailing narrative and assumptions. And if they're brave enough to stick their necks out, as did Harvard's Kuldorff, Oxford's Gupta, and Stanford's Bhattacharya, they're going to cause some disruption, which they did.

It's at moments like this when the question can be answered: what will the globalists do to those who don't agree with them? The answer? They'll try to ruin them. As the *Wall Street Journal* piece reported:

> That didn't please the lockdown consensus enforced by public health officials and the press. Dr. Collins, the director of the National Institutes of Health until Sunday, sent an email on Oct. 8, 2020, to Dr. Fauci, the director of the National Institute of Allergy and Infectious diseases.
>
> "This proposal from the three fringe epidemiologists . . . seems to be getting a lot of attention—and even a cosignature from Nobel Prize winner Mike Leavitt at Stanford. There needs to be a quick and devastating published takedown of its premises," Dr. Collins wrote. "Is it underway?"[6]

It's difficult to read this opinion piece from the *Wall Street Journal* and come away with anything but the impression that these alleged scientists are not any different from warring mafia dons or corporate raiders using underhanded tactics to take down the competition. In the nineteenth century, when there was a dispute over who should be given credit for the theory of natural selection, Charles Darwin or Alfred Russel Wallace, a public debate was held in London, England, by the Linnean Society on July 1, 1858, to settle the question.

Would it have been so difficult in 2020 to have these scientists debate the issue of lockdowns and other public health measures on a three-hour public Zoom call? Millions would have tuned into that debate, and we would have all been better informed. The *Wall Street Journal* opinion piece continued their critique:

These researchers weren't fringe and neither was their opposition to quarantining society. But in the panic over the virus, these two voices of science used their authority to stigmatize dissenters and crush debate. A week after his email, Dr. Collins spoke to the *Washington Post* about the Great Barrington Declaration. "This is a fringe component of epidemiology," he said. "This is not mainstream science. It's dangerous." His message spread and the alternative strategy was dismissed in most precincts.[7]

This effort by Collins and Fauci can seem puzzling to the average person, but when you view it through the lens of globalism and Technocracy, the idea that scientists, engineers, and managers are best situated to make the important decisions in society, it all becomes clear.

They don't believe in free and open debate because they don't trust you to make the right decision. This becomes remarkably clear in a bizarre statement made by Dr. Fauci as he found himself under attack by a few brave Republicans and media outlets:

> On CBS, Dr. Fauci said Republicans who criticize him are "really criticizing science, because I represent science. That's dangerous." He isn't "science." And it's also dangerous for scientific officials to mobilize to quash dissent, without which it's easy to make tragic mistakes. A scientific debate over pandemic policy was and still is in the public interest, especially during a once-in-a-century plague . . .
>
> . . . Rather than try to manipulate public opinion, the job of health officials is to offer their best scientific advice. They shouldn't act like politicians or censors, and when they do, they squander the public's trust.[8]

It's articles like this one from the *Wall Street Journal* that confirm my belief that much more was going on with COVID-19 than we were led to believe. Fauci and Collins strike me as little different than the generals who lied about our progress on Vietnam, Iraq, and Afghanistan.

For the sake of clarity, let me tell you what I consider to be the most likely explanations for what happened during the COVID-19 crisis.

I consider the most likely scenario to be that COVID-19 was released on purpose by the globalists to terrify us into accepting their authoritarian rule, complete with dangerous vaccines that would kill or maim a large part of the population, requiring further government support.

I consider the second-most likely scenario to be that there was an accidental escape of this pathogen from the Wuhan Institute of Virology, and the globalists saw it as an opportunity to implement their long-cherished plans of global governance.

I consider the least likely scenario to be that this was somehow a natural outbreak in Wuhan, China (especially since the bats who carry the precursor to this virus lived hundreds of miles away), and that the authorities and globalists were taking the measures they did because they genuinely believed they were justified by the unprecedented nature of the emergency.

In what follows I will not argue for scenario number one or two, even though I believe either to be the most likely explanation. When people engage in horrendous violations of the public's trust, as they did during the Vietnam War, Iraq, and Afghanistan, it can take decades before the majority of the public sees the truth clearly.

Nobody likes to believe they've been betrayed by their leaders.

It isn't because people are stupid that they believe so many of the lies of our ruling class. It's because they're good people who get up and do the hard work of society with honor and dignity. They cannot imagine the minds of those who do not do the same.

They require an overwhelming amount of evidence to finally accept that certain people are evil.

Therefore, I'm not going to deal with the question of whether SARS-CoV-2 was a man-made organism, released either intentionally or by accident.

I am going to treat the COVID-19 crisis as an Act of God, like an earthquake or flood, and show you that even under this generous interpretation, the globalists have embraced a terrifying plan for humanity's future.

* * *

The lockdowns in our country started in March 2020, but on July 9, 2020, Klaus Schwab (with a new coauthor, Terry Mallert) published a new book, *COVID-19: The Great Reset*, searching desperately for a way to rebrand his globalist agenda.

The "Fourth Industrial Revolution" never took off as a catchy idea, so maybe "The Great Reset" would have more luck.

However, Klaus Schwab couldn't avoid his tendency to engage in literary gee-whiz, "ain't technology brought to you by really smart people great?" And did I mention we need a new political system to handle all these changes? Let's start with the cheery introduction:

> At the time of writing (June 2020), the pandemic continues to worsen globally. Many of us are pondering when things will return to normal. Nothing will ever return to the "broken" sense of normalcy that prevailed prior to the crisis because the coronavirus pandemic marks a fundamental inflection point in our global trajectory. Some analysts call it a major bifurcation, others refer to a deep crisis of "biblical" proportions, but the essence remains the same: the world as we knew it in the early months of 2020 is no more, dissolved in the context of the pandemic.[9]

We're now more than two years past the time Schwab was writing, and I want you to think about how he claims the world has forever changed. Let me ask you. Are you still married to the same person? Do your dogs still need to be walked and does the litterbox for the cat still need to be emptied? Much of your life probably seems the same, except for the insane people wearing their masks as they drive alone in their cars, or the expensive gas and the inflation at the supermarkets.

But that's not because of COVID-19.

Those are man-made problems, brought about by bad decisions at the top level of our government, and you don't need to be an insurrectionist to believe that.

Schwab doesn't even claim that the world before the pandemic was good, as shown by snarky lines like "Nothing will ever return to the 'broken' sense of normalcy that prevailed prior to the crisis." Can somebody who isn't clinically insane tell me what's meant by that line? You thought the time before the pandemic was normal, but in reality, it was "broken." Is that like the old joke about there being no such thing as "military intelligence," "business ethics," or "jumbo shrimp"?

The book is divided into three sections, with the first being titled "Macro Reset." You see, it wasn't enough to just be a "Reset," or even a "Great Reset." It had to be a "Macro Reset" to really get your attention! See how skillfully you're being manipulated by really smart people?

And who is coming to save the day? It's not any single person. It's Big Government. What a surprise!

> In the words of John Micklethwait and Adrian Woolridge: "The COVID-19 pandemic has made government important again. Not just powerful again (look at those once-mighty companies begging for help), but also vital again: It matters enormously whether your country has a good health service, competent bureaucrats, and sound finances. Good government is the difference between living and dying."
>
> One of the great lessons of the past five centuries in Europe and America is this: acute crises contribute to boosting the power of the state. It's always been the case and there is no reason why it should be different with COVID-19.[10]

Wait just a Texas minute, there. Can you believe Klaus Schwab is saying that in every acute crisis of the past five centuries in Europe or America, it was the governments that provided the solution? These people do not like individual action or achievement. Their hatred for strong individuals literally oozes out of them. How about this line, "look at those once-mighty companies begging for help." Does that seem like something a psychologically well-balanced person would say?

And just for my sake, can anybody point me to a single country in the history of the world that can be said to have had "competent bureaucrats"? To me it seems that the best life is achieved by maximum avoidance of any government bureaucrats. I'll take sending a package from the UPS Store over a US Postal Office any day of the week, even if it costs me a little more. Efficiency matters, and we shouldn't grumble if we have to pay a little more for it.

Schwab's intention in writing these books seems to be to make you feel powerless and beg for his chain of authority to be placed around your neck so you can be ridden like some domesticated animal. Consider how optimistic and upbeat you feel after reading this passage:

> If no one power can enforce order, our world will suffer from a "global order deficit." Unless individual nations and international organizations succeed in finding solutions to better collaborate at the global level, we risk entering an "age of entropy" in which retrenchment, fragmentation, anger and parochialism will increasingly define our global landscape, making it less intelligible and more disorderly. The pandemic crisis has both exposed and exacerbated this sad state of affairs. The magnitude and consequence of the shock it has inflicted are such that *no extreme scenario can now be taken off the table* (italics added by author).[11]

It's taken two and a half books, but Schwab, in the middle of the COVID-19 crisis, laid out his plan to deal with the dissidents.

"No extreme scenario can now be taken off the table."

What might those extreme scenarios be?

The shutting down of opposing voices on social media?

Deleting a person's email list?

Cutting off a person's access to financial payment services?

Denying banking services to an individual because of their political beliefs?

Using law enforcement agencies, like the FBI or IRS, to harass the dissidents?

The creation of detention camps, to be utilized for those who deny health mandates, or simply protest the plans of the government?

The mass execution of those who defy government orders?

Do any of these seem too extreme? Schwab himself wrote that "no extreme scenario can now be taken off the table."

When people tell you their plans, I suggest you listen to what they say. I cannot presume the slightest bit of goodwill when Schwab writes that "no extreme scenario can now be taken off the table." It's like hiring an employee who tells you he's been fired from his previous jobs because all his bosses were jerks, or starting to date a woman who tells you she's "never quite managed the monogamy thing." When the end comes, you really shouldn't be so surprised.

However, like a frog being slowly cooked to death in a pot of water placed over a low flame, you might not notice the creeping heat of global tyranny until it's too late. That's why you probably need Schwab to put it all in perspective for you:

> Global governance is commonly defined as the process of cooperation among transnational actors aimed at providing responses to global problems (those that affect more than one state or region). It encompasses the totality of institutions, policies, norms, procedures, and initiatives through which nation states try to bring more predictability and stability to their responses to transnational challenges. This definition makes it clear that any global effort on any global issue or concern is bound to be toothless without the cooperation of national governments and their ability to act and legislate their aims.[12]

Color me skeptical, but I'm not seeing Schwab put any limits on what governments can do to their citizens, or the pressure to be applied to average people by "institutions, policies, norms, procedures, and initiatives." Their plans sound reminiscent of some take-it-or-leave-it Big Tech contract when you want their new phone, computer, or app.

The best-case scenario if you defy them is you might end up without an Internet connection, a phone, a bank account, or a job.

From history we have learned the worst-case scenario for those who defy authoritarian control. They end up in jail, brutally tortured, and often dead.

As we continue, I will show you exactly how Klaus Schwab and his cronies are putting in just such a system.

They want you to believe it's for your own good, or it's for the children, or to save the sea turtles.

They know better than you do because they're smart.

* * *

And whom did Schwab choose to praise in the COVID-19 crisis?

Not the scientific dissidents, such as those who signed the Great Barrington Declaration, who would never have sent elderly people with the virus back into nursing homes. The same dissidents who would have made the decision to allow the use of drugs like hydroxychloroquine and ivermectin, given their decades-long history of safe usage, likely saving the lives of hundreds of thousands in the United States and millions around the globe.

No. That didn't happen.

Klaus Schwab saw fit to praise the Chinese. Yes, the same Chinese communists who in all likelihood created the virus, and then allowed for its spread by locking down internal travel from Wuhan, while allowing it to the rest of the world. The same Chinese communists whose opening to the world was led by globalists Henry Kissinger and Zbigniew Brzezinski. Kissinger and Brzezinski saw fit to teach the Chinese how to set up an economy run by scientists, engineers, and managers, while at the same time depriving their citizens of any political freedoms. The Chinese citizens could have a fat belly and an expensive car, but they'd better have an empty head when it came to criticizing their leaders.

From Schwab's *COVID-19:The Great Reset*:

> All these prompted Kishore Mahbubani, an influential analyst of the rivalry that opposes the US and China, to argue that COVID-19 has reversed the roles of both countries in terms of dealing with disasters and supporting others. While in the past the US was always the first to arrive with aid where assistance was needed (like on 26 December 2004 when a major tsunami hit Indonesia), this role now belongs to China, he says. In March 2020, China sent to Italy 31 tons of medical equipment (ventilators, masks, and protective suits) that the EU could not provide . . . Mahbubani says that it is their choices [China and the US] that will determine who wins the rivalry contest and that those will be based on "the cold calculus of reason to work out cost-benefit analyses of what both the U.S. and China have to offer them."[13]

Does it sound like Schwab has a nation-crush on China? It does to me. As others have already said, the globalists love China. It has enabled them to put their ideas into practice on a massive scale without regard to human rights. Like our Founding Fathers, I believe our rights are an inheritance from God, who loves us above all things, and the attempt to create a society devoid of such rights strikes me as truly of the devil.

I wish I didn't have to resort to such extreme language. But if I didn't, I'd be lying to you. I'm telling you what I think. We are not just the physical.

All of us have to answer for our actions in this world. We are spirit, and the attempt to deny such a reality is the path to suffering and hell. Look at history and tell me I'm wrong. The fascists of Italy, the Nazis of Germany, and the communists of the Soviet Union all sought to restrict the rights of people and placed the government as their god.

When ideologues get in charge and tell you they must "temporarily" do terrible things, the atrocities just keep piling up.

It's as predictable as the law of gravity.

As was this comment from Schwab about how the pandemic, in which millions around the world died unnecessarily, should be viewed as an opportunity by those concerned about climate change:

> Some leaders and decision-makers who were already at the forefront of the fight against climate change may want to take advantage of the shock inflicted by the pandemic to inflict long-lasting and wider environmental changes. They will, in effect, make "good use" of the pandemic by not letting the crisis go to waste. [A famous statement attributed to Chicago mayor and Obama Chief of Staff Rahm Emanuel.] The exhortation of different leaders ranging from HRH the Prince of Wales to Andrew Cuomo to "build back better" goes in that direction.[14]

As I've said before, the answer to any question for these globalists seems to be more globalism. Got a pandemic? How about managing it badly, then claiming you need a more powerful government for the next time? These people really are shameless.

Schwab also probably didn't realize that Governor Andrew Cuomo of New York would resign in shame on August 24, 2021, under a cloud of sexual assault allegations, likely scuttling any chance he had of becoming president of the United States in either 2024 or 2028. Maybe Schwab is betting on Prince Charles becoming King of England, where he will most likely be the least popular king in English history.

I sometimes wonder if Klaus Schwab gets angry that he just can't find any good henchmen. That is the universal problem of most villains throughout history. It seems that idiocy is just part of the typical operating system of your average globalist.

But not to worry. Like any good supervillain, the globalists don't like to brood on past failures but instead always look forward to the next wonder weapon, like a laser to blow up the moon, or in the real world, digital surveillance, to finally achieve that long-desired control over humanity:

> Now that information and communication technologies permeate almost every aspect of our lives and forms of social participation, any digital experience that we have can be turned into a "product" designed to monitor and anticipate our behavior. The risk of dystopia stems from this observation . . . In academia, it finds its expression in the research undertaken by scholars like Shoshana Zuboff. Her book *Surveillance Capitalism* warns about customers being reinvented as data sources, with "surveillance capitalism" transforming our economy, politics, society and our own lives by producing deeply anti-democratic asymmetries of knowledge and the power that accrues to knowledge.[15]

In plain language, that means when the government knows everything about you, then you are at their mercy. That's called an "asymmetry of knowledge." In a better world, you know all about the government, but they know little about you. Klaus Schwab really doesn't like that world and makes it clear. It's probably not a surprise that Schwab would turn to his favorite globalist academic, Yuval Noah Harari, in order to justify this new tool. He quotes the Harari argument at length:

> Surveillance technology is developing at breakneck speed, and what seemed science fiction 10 years ago is today old news. As a thought experiment, consider a hypothetical government that demands that every citizen wears a biometric bracelet that monitors body temperature and heart rate 24 hours a day. The resulting data is hoarded and analyzed by government algorithms. The algorithms will know that you are sick even before you know it, and they will also know where you have been, and who you have met. The chains of infection could be drastically shortened, and even cut altogether.[16]

In fairness to Harari's article from March 2020, he does go on to detail the danger of such a system in the hands of a government that could also monitor your enthusiasm at a political rally or while watching certain shows, but the discussion doesn't seem to go any further.

As an observation, I must note a pattern I've noticed in Schwab's work: he seems to acknowledge the arguments of the other side but never really addresses them. He strikes me much like that boss who pretends to acknowledge the complaints of his employees but never fights against upper management over their decisions.

In Schwab's case, though, he's just pretending to be the manager.

He's really angling to be the boss.

He wants to be the one you complain to about being fired, but in reality, he's the one who made the decision.

* * *

Another example of how Schwab and his globalist allies try to pit both sides against each other comes in the next section on governments and business. In this section, he tries to sound like a conservative:

> For all the reasons expanded upon in the first chapter, COVID-19 has rewritten many of the rules of the game between the public and private sectors. In the post-pandemic era, business will be subject to much greater governmental interference than in the past. The benevolent (or otherwise) greater intrusion of governments in the life of companies and the conduct of their business will be country-and-industry dependent, therefore taking many different guises.[17]

This might strike you as the initial setup of a conservative speaker. But it's not. This is the opening gambit of a fascist. Sure, Schwab wants to use the government for a while to achieve his aims, but then toss it overboard when his corporate buddies can fully implement their plans.

And right on cue, Schwab comes up with his new idea: stakeholder capitalism. It will sound like he wants to be more democratic. He doesn't. It's just a trick to get more power into the hands of his buddies:

> The pandemic struck at a time when many different issues, ranging from climate change activism and rising inequalities to gender diversity and #MeToo scandals, had already begun to raise awareness and heighten the criticality of stakeholder capitalism and ESG [environmental, social, and governance] considerations in today's interdependent world. Whether espoused openly or not, nobody can deny that companies' fundamental purpose can no longer be simply the unbridled pursuit of financial profit; it is now incumbent upon them to serve all their stakeholders, not only those who hold shares.[18]

Remember when I said that the globalists will use any issue to promote their plans? There's COVID-19, climate change, inequality, gender diversity, and now the #MeToo movement, all part of the globalist plan to create maximum chaos and fear, the better to implement their authoritarian agenda.

The issue really doesn't matter because the answer is always the same: globalism.

In the world of the globalists, the pattern is always the same: the individual must be overruled by the power of the group, inevitably led by Schwab and his buddies. This is from a section of Schwab's COVID-19 book on the need for everybody to undergo an individual reset:

> Psychologists tell us that cognitive closure often calls for black-and-white thinking and simplistic solutions—a terrain propitious for conspiracy theorists and the propagation of rumors, fake news, mistruths, and other pernicious ideas. In such a context, we look for leadership, authority and clarity, meaning that the

question as to whom to trust (within our immediate community and among our leaders) becomes critical. In consequence, so too does the countervailing issue of whom we distrust.[19]

For all their supposed brilliance, it's remarkable how little these globalists seem to want to engage in any type of intellectual debate. They simply want to prevent any debate from happening. The only question seems to be who has the authority to speak. After that we're supposed to believe the words that spill from the mouth as if we were listening to the voice of God.

When one is starting a relationship with a domestic abuser, the behavior can look much different from when one is deep into the relationship. People do not get into abusive relationships because they want to be harmed. It's because they're persuaded. The new person is charming, attentive, passionate, all things that may have seemed to be missing from the other person's life.

But once the relationship is set, once there is some sort of commitment, the abuse can begin. The abusive acts will not be seen as common, but as an anomaly.

"Oh, that happened because he hadn't gotten much sleep the night before."

Or "That fight wouldn't have happened if that other guy hadn't been checking me out."

However, the actions tell you the truth. This is Schwab being persuasive to you, hoping you'll join with him:

> The deep crisis provoked by the pandemic has given us plenty of opportunities to reflect on how our economies and societies work and the ways in which they don't. The verdict seems clear: we need to change; we should change. But can we? Will we learn from the mistakes in the past? Will the pandemic open the door to a better future? Will we get our global house in order? Simply put, will we put into motion the Great Reset?[20]

What is Schwab giving us other than a call to action with no substance behind it? It sounds warm and cozy, and yet it's maddeningly vague. At least when the television preachers give you such a pitch, they helpfully give you a phone number to call so you can pledge your money.

But you need to be aware of how Schwab plans to get to that good place. I don't want you to forget for a second the line in which he wrote, "No extreme scenario can now be taken off the table."

With that quote fresh in your mind, I want you to consider the following passage from the conclusion of *COVID-19: The Great Reset:*

> The absolute prerequisite for a proper reset is greater collaboration
> and cooperation within and between countries. Cooperation—a
> "supremely human cognitive ability" that put our species on its
> unique and extraordinary trajectory—can be summed up as
> "shared intentionality" to act together towards a common goal.
> We simply cannot progress without it.[21]

When I read that passage, I'm filled with fear. This is the key. They want your cooperation, just like the vampire of legend needs an invitation to cross the threshold of a house. The globalists want you to invite them into your lives.

The globalists keep focusing on the words "collaboration and cooperation" because they don't want you to think about those who raise questions, the dissidents. The globalists don't like individuals or individual accomplishments because they prevent them from taking control behind a facade of "all the people want this outcome." Just think back to your high school years and what the adults told you about avoiding peer pressure to engage in activities that might be harmful to yourself or others, like drag racing down the street at 120 miles per hour.

Sure, you might have succumbed a few times to the peer pressure. But your older and wiser self asks, "How the hell did I survive to adulthood?" That's probably why the wildest kids turn into the strictest parents, because they know how easy it is to do stupid things. This is what Schwab wrote on the last page of his COVID-19 book, to make sure that if you disagree with him, you realize you're not one of the cool kids at school:

> These expressions of individual hope are supported by a multitude of surveys concluding that we collectively desire change. They range from a poll in the UK showing that a majority of people want to fundamentally alter the economy as it recovers, in contrast to one-fourth wanting it to return to how it was, to international surveys finding that a large majority of citizens around the world want the economic recovery from the corona virus to prioritize climate change and to support a green recovery. Worldwide, movements demanding a "better future" and calling for a shift to an economic system that prioritizes our collective well-being over mere GDP growth are proliferating.[22]

Do you get it? Everybody is demanding a better world. Get with the program. You don't want to be left behind. You might be forced to eat your lunch all by yourself in the high school cafeteria.

But you know that's never how it goes when the uptight-know-it-alls try to run a school. That's because you've got the stoners, the car heads, and the jocks, and they can't stand the brown-noser, student council, perfect kids who cry if they don't get a hundred percent on every test. It's why the globalists are going after the disruptive people, like Dave Chapelle, Ricky Gervais, or Elon Musk. They can't stand anybody making fun of them.

If that happens, Klaus Schwab and his goons, under the rubric of "No extreme scenario can now be taken off the table," are likely to take you behind the gymnasium and beat the hell out of you, or even worse.

*  *  *

Did you think the easing of the COVID-19 crisis would lessen the maniacal plans of the globalists?

The World Economic Forum at Davos was canceled in 2021 and held virtually in January 2022, but they decided by May 2022 that it was safe for them to once again meet in person. This is how it was depicted in the media:

> The WEF 2022 is meeting in springtime rather than January—when it is traditionally held—for the first time, having been postponed on multiple occasions by COVID-19.
>
> Besides the novelty that the change of season brings, the WEF is meeting at a crucial time.
>
> In its 50-year history the WEF has never been confronted with such unprecedented global issues as it now faces in 2022, as the world recovers from a global pandemic, grapples to contain the devastating impact of the climate crisis and navigates a geopolitical storm following the invasion of Ukraine.[23]

For the globalists it's always five seconds to midnight on the doomsday clock, and they're the only ones who can save us. If you're wondering what might transpire at a typical meeting of the World Economic Forum at Davos, let's look at what happened in 2022.

On May 18, Klaus Schwab held a talk with eager journalists who wanted to know what was going to be on the agenda for the globalists:

> "In a world which is becoming more fragmented, more divided, and where many of the traditional multilateral organizations tend to become dysfunctional, or at least mistrustful, a global platform based on informal, trust-faced and action-oriented cooperation will be ever more relevant, more important than before," Schwab declared.
>
> More than 50 heads of state and government will attend the meeting next week, including NATO Secretary general Jens Stoltenberg, German Chancellor Olaf Schloz, and Ursula von der Leyen, President of the European Commission, the WEF lists.[24]

Schwab may have wanted to present a warm and welcoming appearance to the rest of the world, but he wasted little time in letting people know that if they didn't behave, he was ready to use an iron fist.

Schwab warned anyone who sought to trivialize the event or hijack its key messages, including the often-mentioned Great Reset, will be treated with contempt.

Contrary voices will simply not be tolerated.

"The atmosphere in which Davos takes place will be welcoming. But it is also of utmost seriousness," he confided. "So, there's no place for the frivolous fringe that seeks to distract and divert attention. And I condemn it wholeheartedly, particularly of those who have nothing to do with the World Economic Forum, community, and just come to Davos to hijack our brand."[25]

It's a little disheartening to realize that more than fifty heads of state, as well as many more high government officials and heads of industry, attended an event that is so hostile to free speech.

But Davos 2022 wasn't going to limit its disapproval of free speech to comments by their fearless leader. Many of the participants seemed eager to follow Schwab's anti-free speech agenda, such as Australia's E-Safety commissioner, Julie Inman Grant:

> Speaking to the WEF Panel on Monday, commissioner Julie Inman Grant spoke of the need to rethink various rights, including the right to free speech.
>
> "We are finding ourselves in a place where we have increasing polarization everywhere, and everything feels binary, when it doesn't need to be," Inman Grant said.
>
> "So I think we're going to have to think about a recalibration of a whole range of human rights that are playing out online, from the freedom of speech to be[ing] free from online violence," she added.[26]

The current Australian government seems to be committed to a "recalibration" of free speech. That is a truly terrifying idea, as we know it means they will seek to ban or limit any speech that affects their political power. There can be little question that this is exactly what they are seeking.

If one wonders if this is the actual plan, one need only consider what happened to journalist Jack Posobiec, probably one of the most effective and popular of the Davos critics:

> Heavily armed Swiss officers, appearing from the Ordnungsdienst police force, allegedly "frisked" and detained Human Events Daily host and Turning Point USA contributor Jack Posobiec on Monday afternoon.
>
> The officers, who also told independent journalist Savannah Hernandez not to film them, claimed they have a right not to be filmed in Switzerland, despite there not appearing to be a federal law prohibiting people from filming police.[27]

This is typical for the globalists, who don't seem to let a little thing like the lack of a law prevent them from exercising their will. They apparently exist above any national laws.

If you want a more authoritative take, one only had to wait for the talk by Susan Wojciki, the CEO of YouTube (now owned by Google). The article from *Fortune* magazine opened with this:

> It's a precarious time for tech CEOs whose businesses have to juggle misinformation, free speech, and demands from employees to take a stand on global and domestic issues. For YouTube CEO Susan Wojciki, those responsibilities come on top of her efforts to grow the company with new competitors vying for screen time, the war in Ukraine, and an economic downturn that many predict will become a recession.[28]

Poor Susan Wojciki. It can be so difficult to be a "Master of the Universe" when the peasants don't appreciate what you're doing.

Helpfully, Wojciki tries to explain her thinking to the crowd at Davos, and the barbarians beyond the gates:

> "There are a number of different ways we can look at this," she said. "The first would be from a policy standpoint. We would look at content that we would think about in terms of being violative of our policies."
>
> If you look at COVID, she suggested, YouTube came up with 10 different policies that the platform said would be deemed violating—like saying that COVID came from something other than a virus. Wojciki said YouTube did see people attacking 5G equipment because they thought it was causing COVID. That would be an example of content that would be removed.
>
> The second viewpoint, she continued, would be raising up authoritative information. "If you are dealing with a sensitive subject like news, health, science, we are going to make sure that what we're recommending is coming from a trusted, well-known publisher that can be reliable."[29]

It is genuinely remarkable that, in this day and age where we have the best educated populace in our history, these Big Tech companies believe they must resort to such censorship. The old understanding that good ideas will win over bad ideas in the marketplace of thought has been replaced by a mistrust of robust debate. The new answer seems to be to "trust the experts," even if they're the ones who might have caused the problem or are profiting from the crisis.

Besides destroying the centuries-old practice of free speech and empowering dictators to control information, there were new innovations introduced at Davos, like your own personal carbon footprint tracker, brought to you by the enlightened communist masters of China:

> Speaking at a "Strategic Outlook: Responsible Consumption" WEF Panel in Davos, Alibaba Group President J. Michael Evans

said that his company will be introducing more surveillance systems within China in order to usher in a so-called greener future.

"We are developing through technology the ability for consumers to measure their own carbon footprint . . . where they are traveling, how they are traveling, what they are eating, what they are consuming on the platform," Evans said . . .

Evans did not disclose if the data would be shared with the government, however, like with all Chinese corporations, Alibaba is beholden by law to provide data to the CCP, as it was reportedly pressured to do so in January of last year.[30]

Imagine that. China has another way to surveil its citizens. As we have already discussed, China has been the experimental lab of the globalists for decades. How long will it be before Democrats in the United States will be calling for all of us to have these trackers? I imagine it won't be long. Maybe two or three years.

But while you may find yourself interested in the attack of free speech, or surveillance of your carbon footprint, you might be saying to yourself, I wonder what George Soros is doing these days? Well, even though he's ninety-one years old, he decided to show up at the World Economic Forum in Davos in 2022 to give his thoughts:

Billionaire George Soros warned that Russia's invasion of Ukraine had rattled Europe and could be the start of another world war.

"Other issues that concern all of humanity—fighting pandemics and climate change, avoiding nuclear war, maintaining global institutions—have had to take a back seat to that struggle," Soros, 91, said Tuesday at the World Economic Forum in Davos, Switzerland. "That's why I say our civilization may not survive."[31]

Isn't it good to know that if you or I portentously say, "Civilization may not survive," the media will attack us as calling for our listeners to stage an insurrection? But if you're George Soros and have billions of dollars, when you say the exact same thing, you're treated as a wise sage.

However, predictions by Soros are often so wrong that one might be tempted to bet against anything he says. In 2020, this was what Soros was warning:

> Soros has previously used the WEF stage to unleash blistering critiques. At the last meeting, in January 2020, he suggested without evidence that Facebook Inc. might be conspiring to help re-elect Donald Trump, who lost the US presidency later that year.[32]

If that's what Soros was complaining about in 2020, I'm likely to believe that civilization has a very bright future. I'll listen to Soros and immediately translate it into the opposite.

And what globalist meeting wouldn't be complete without Bill Gates talking about vaccines?

> A partnership between U.S. drug maker Pfizer and the Bill and Melinda Gates Foundation to speed up the development of vaccines to prevent diseases that cause newborn mortality would also advance efforts to make a high-tech malaria vaccine, Bill Gates said at the World Economic Forum in Davos on Wednesday.
>
> Pfizer and the foundation will also work with Rwanda, Malawi and other African countries to increase access to all of the company's medicines and vaccines for their populations.
>
> "[We have] a dream for [beating] malaria, and we'll talk to the great mRNA companies, including Pfizer, about this . . . we could use that mRNA platform to make a really powerful malaria vaccine," Mr. Gates said.[33]

Yes, Bill Gates loves his vaccines. And he is an enthusiastic participant at the World Economic Forum, where he gets to rub shoulders with the other rich and powerful people of the world.

It would be so much easier not to call Klaus Schwab and his assorted friends around the world an evil, globalist cabal trying to change humanity, if they stopped acting like one. But it appears they can't help telling people exactly what they are. This is how Schwab's opening address to the World Economic Forum on May 23, 2022, was reported:

> On the evidence delivered on day one at the famous Swiss ski resort, Schwab very much sees his organization at the forefront of shaping the world of tomorrow.
>
> Unfortunately, outsiders have not been consulted or invited to join the 2,500 people flown in from all around the world to be present.
>
> Schwab was quick to praise those gathered before him in his welcoming address.
>
> "The future is not just happening. The future is built by us, by a powerful community, as you here in this room. We have the means to improve the state of the world . . ."[34]

This is the game that Klaus Schwab and his cronies play. They don't want you to criticize their plans, but then they go around bragging about their plans to change the world, and their strength.

But remember what they say about those who stand in their way.

"No extreme scenario can now be taken off the table."

It is time for us to finally see the globalists for who they are and what they want to do, behind all their smoke-and-mirror tricks.

## Chapter Five

# Yuval Noah Harari—Robocop for the Empire

There can be little doubt that Klaus Schwab loves to quote Israeli academic and writer Yuval Noah Harari. Dr. Patrick Wood told me I should consider Harari "the brain of Klaus Schwab,"[1] and many claim he is Schwab's top adviser.[2]

Harari is best known for his million-copy bestsellers, which seem to find great favor with the most powerful people in the world. The front of the paperback version of his book *Sapiens* has an endorsement from Bill Gates that reads, "I would recommend *Sapiens* to anyone who's interested in the history and future of our species."

Gates also helpfully provided an endorsement for *21 Lessons for the 21st Century*, writing, "Offers a helpful framework for processing the news and thinking about challenges we face."

This is how Harari is described on his page for Klaus Schwab's World Economic Forum:

Historian, philosopher, and the author of the bestsellers "Sapiens: A Brief History of Humanity", "Homo Deus: A Brief History of Tomorrow", and "21 Lessons for the 21st Century". Co-Founder of Sapienship, a multidisciplinary organization advocating for global responsibility whose mission is to clarify the public conversation, support the quest for solutions and focus attention on the most important challenges facing the world today (technological disruption, ecological collapse and the nuclear threat). 2002, PhD, University of Oxford, Lecturer, department of History, Hebrew University of Jerusalem. Books have sold more than 20 million copies worldwide. Research focuses on macro-historical questions such as: What is the relationship between history and biology? What is the essential difference between Homo sapiens and other animals? Is there justice in history?[3]

There can be little doubt of Harari's intelligence. But what of his judgment? Is he wise in how he approaches things? Karl Marx was certainly of high intelligence, as his critique of nineteenth-century capitalism can still strike us as containing great truth. And yet communism has been responsible for untold suffering around the world.

Like Marx, Harari seeks to remake society, professing a unique reinterpretation of history, which better suits his aims. It has been said that if you control the past, you can control the future. The first task before Harari is to convince you that your understanding of the past is flawed, and once he convinces you of that, it will be so much easier to move you to his desired future.

When Schwab and his fellow globalists like to speak to people, they don't start with their plans. They like to lull you into a sense of wonder by telling you a lot of things you might not know. And giving credit where credit is due, Harari is a first-class collector of esoteric, interesting information. However, it's his interpretation that is problematic, and I suspect even his fellow historians are probably aghast at his penchant for sweeping generalizations.

In Harari's view, it would seem the greatest tool at the hand of the globalists is the story, the narrative, or mythology that supports a society. In his book *Sapiens*, he confronts the question of how people collaborated to build the pyramids of Egypt. He writes of the problems that develop when technology allows for a population to move beyond the hunter-gatherer stage and live in villages or cities:

> ... The mere fact that one can feed a thousand people in the same town or a million people in the same kingdom does not guarantee that they can agree how to divide the land and water, how to settle disputes and conflicts, and how to act in times of drought or war. And if no agreement can be reached, strife spreads, even if the storehouses are bulging. It was not food shortages that caused most of history's wars and revolutions. The French Revolution was spearheaded by affluent lawyers, not by famished peasants. The Roman Republic reached the height of its power in the first century, B.C., when treasure fleets from throughout the Mediterranean enriched the Romans beyond their ancestors' wildest dreams. Yet it was at that moment of maximum affluence that the Roman political order collapsed into a series of deadly civil wars.[4]

For the typical reader (myself included), I find that to be a fascinating, thoughtful paragraph. Harari raises an interesting possibility, namely, that revolutions often start in times of relative prosperity.

This idea deserves further exploration.

But rather than exploring the possibilities, Harari wants to give you his answer and make you believe it. Indeed, it doesn't appear as if he's an academic interested in exploring possibilities, but a propagandist for a certain point of view, wanting to convince you to join his merry band:

> The problem at the root of such calamities is that humans evolved for millions of years in small bands of a few dozen individuals. The handful of millennia separating the Agricultural Revolution from the appearance of cities, kingdoms and empires was not enough time to allow an instinct for mass cooperation to evolve.

Despite the lack of such biological instincts, during the forag-
ing era, hundreds of people were able to cooperate thanks to their
shared myths. However, this cooperation was loose and limited.[5]

In my opinion, this is where Harari starts to go off the rails. Or if
you want to take a less charitable view, this is when he reveals how he
wants to brainwash you. Does Harari genuinely believe that the French
Revolution and the Fall of the Roman Republic were due to a failure
of mass cooperation and that if these cultures only had a shared myth,
they'd have survived their challenges? That seems like an enormous
leap of logic, and one that most traditional historians would vigorously
challenge. In this vein, it's interesting to read Harari's critical acclaim
and see how few of his endorsements come from academic historians.

Indeed, it seems to come mostly from the ranks of the elite who
might find themselves at a meeting of the World Economic Forum at
Davos, Switzerland.

\* \* \*

Harari opens the door to asking the question of how people cooperated
when they were members of a hunter-gatherer community. He asserts
this is because they had "shared myths." Did he not consider the possibility that if they did not cooperate, they were likely to perish? The
typical hunter-gatherer community often lived on the razor edge of
survival.

In this context, I find myself agreeing with Harari that in these
communities, decision making was likely to be "loose and limited."
Let's simply assume that to be true. I return to the parable that started
this book, the parable of Thaag and Uther, the leader and the thinker.

Let's imagine our small band living in a temporary village during
the last Ice Age when word spreads through the village that a saber-
tooth cat has been seen prowling around the outskirts. The reports say
the cat seems to be thin and undernourished.

Thaag immediately wants to spring into action, saying, "It must be an old cat who can't hunt for regular food, and that's why he's coming close to the village. Let's get a few men together and kill it."

But Uther has a different idea. "It might be a mother with young cubs nearby. Maybe she looks thin because she's been feeding her cubs. If it's a mother, we'll need more than just a few warriors. Let's get a group together to observe, then we can decide what we need to do."

Again, a dialogue between the leaders and thinkers of the tribe comes up with a better, safer plan. It could be argued that the philosophy with which the United States was founded respects the wisdom of the "loose and limited" cooperation of a typical hunter-gatherer tribe. The best formulation I've heard of the concept of the United States is that we have "majority rule, but minority rights." There are certain tasks in which it is essential to take action, such as building roads, taxes, providing education for the young, or having a military (although we have decided a volunteer military is preferrable to a draft), but in most things we let people make their own decisions.

Harari accepts the idea that it was "loose and limited" cooperation that enabled the success of the hunter-gatherer tribes, allowing them to settle in villages, then cities, and establish nations. The missing component in Harari's analysis is he does not seem to consider the possibility that it was the rise of people like himself, those who think they know better than others, that has caused so much strife as groups of people began to live in larger and larger communities.

Harari argues that as groups of people became larger, the only thing holding them together was some sort of shared myth. Let's be honest about what Harari means when he says the word "myth." In Harari's estimation, "myths" is just another word for "lies," and yet he believes them to be socially useful fabrications.

I believe it's in understanding exactly how Harari is defining words that it's made clear what a tyrannical, dystopian world he wants to create. This is how he dismisses the Declaration of Independence:

Their Declaration of Independence proclaimed universal and eternal principles of justice, which like those of Hammurabi, were inspired by a divine power. However, the most important principle dictated by the American god was somewhat different from the principle dictated by the gods of Babylon. The American Declaration of Independence asserts that:

We hold these truths to be self-evident, that all men are created equal, that they are endowed by their creator with certain unalienable rights, that among these are life, liberty, and the pursuit of happiness.[6]

Harari's language puts me in anticipation that he's going to make the argument that the principles of the American Revolution bear little difference from the gods of Babylon. Which is exactly what he ends up doing, as we shall see.

Harari then commits his most egregious crime against humanity, stripping you of any rights you might have ever believed you possessed:

According to the science of biology, people were not 'created'. They have evolved. And they certainly did not evolve to be 'equal'. The idea of equality is inextricably intertwined with the idea of creation. The Americans got the idea of equality from Christianity, which argues that every person has a divinely created soul, and that all souls are equal before God. However, if we do not believe in the Christian myths about God, creation and souls, what does it mean that all souls are 'equal'? Evolution is based on difference, not on equality.[7]

It's in a paragraph such as this that we can see the true danger of Harari and his fellow globalists. Harari appears to believe the idea of equality sprang from some mystical religious vision of Christianity, rather than the great thinkers of their time observing the human condition and trying to figure out how to get people to live together as peacefully as possible.

I don't have any argument with the idea that in Western civilization much of the advocacy for equality sprang from the Judeo-Christian tradition. But Harari doesn't seem to understand that the concept of every soul being equal before God would find wide acceptance in other religions, such as Hinduism, and that the progress of a free soul, such as in Buddhism, is an essential right of every human being.

Harari continues his unrelenting assault on human rights:

> Similarly, there are no such rights in biology. There are only organs, abilities, and characteristics. Birds fly not because they have a right to fly, but because they have wings. And it's not true that these organs, abilities, and characteristics are 'unalienable'. Many of them undergo constant mutations and may well be completely lost over time. The ostrich is a bird that lost its ability to fly. So 'unalienable rights' should be translated into 'mutable characteristics'.[8]

I don't believe it's too much of a stretch to say this is a paragraph that dangerously flirts with saying that humanity has no essential nature.

Harari goes on to attack the ideas of liberty and happiness (for which he can find no scientific way to measure, therefore concluding it doesn't exist), before offering up his own amended Declaration of Independence from his view of reality:

> So here is that line from the American Declaration of Independence translated into biological terms.
> We hold these truths to be self-evident, that all men evolved differently, that they are born with certain mutable characteristics, that among these are life and the pursuit of pleasure.[9]

In this single passage, Harari tells you the globalist plan. Evolution may have been the original creator rather than God, but the engineers, scientists, and managers of the New World Order will now engage in the work of re-creating man into their own desired image. And they really don't have any plan for your "liberty" in this new world. Harari claims that any order we observe in a society does not reflect reality, or an accepted way of running a society, but is only an example of "imagined order."

In their view, man has no natural state.

Of course, there will be the elite who understand this, but in order for society to function, it's necessary to have a large number of fools ("true believers") who believe the nonsense spouted by the leaders. Harari explains it in the following manner:

> A single priest often does the work of a hundred soldiers—far more cheaply and effectively. Moreover, no matter how efficient bayonets are, somebody must wield them. Why should the soldiers, jailors, judges, and police maintain an imagined order in which they do not believe? Of all human collective activities, the one most difficult to organize is violence. To say that a social order is maintained by a military force immediately raises the question: what maintains the military order? It is impossible to organize an army solely by coercion. At least some of the commanders and soldiers must truly believe in something, be it God, honor, motherland, manhood or money.[10]

Without realizing it, Harari is arguing that man does have a natural state. And in that natural state, humans do not wish to commit violence against others. They need to be organized into an army, dedicated to some principal in order to commit this violence.

* * *

So, if all social order is only "imagined," how do you get people to accept your new and improved order?

You have to be constantly "organizing" the people and continually "educating" them. Becoming a global dictator enforcing your will on the planet's population requires a lot of work. You need to get up early and work late. They don't mention that enough in evil dictator school. Harari explains:

> You also educate people constantly. From the moment they are born, you constantly remind them of the principles of the imagined order, which are incorporated into anything and everything. They are incorporated into fairy tales, dramas, paintings, songs, etiquette, political propaganda, architecture, recipes, and fashions. For example, today people believe in equality, so it's fashionable for rich kids to wear jeans, which were originally working-class attire.[11]

How is Harari striking you now? Are you comfortable with the fact that it appears he's softening you up for an attack on equality? In addition, he wants you to know he's ready to go to war against all the things that you believe.

In place of culture, which Harari seems to hold up as suspect because it upholds the "imagined order" of society, rather than the accumulated wisdom of centuries, Harari wants to celebrate bureaucracy, in a section he titles without even a hint of irony, "The Wonders of Bureaucracy":

> In order to function, the people who operate such a system of drawers must be reprogrammed to stop thinking as humans and start thinking as clerks and accountants. As everyone from ancient times until today knows, clerks and accountants think in a non-human fashion. They think like filing cabinets. This is not their fault. If they don't think that way their drawers will all get mixed up and they won't be able to provide the services their government, company or organization requires. The most important impact of script on human history is precisely this: it has gradually changed the way humans think and view the world. Free association and holistic thought have given way to compartmentalization and bureaucracy.[12]

Are there any accountants out there who might take exception to Harari's claims? The accountants I've known generally seem to be the best judges of human nature because they understand nothing reveals more about a person than where they spend their money.

Rather than being disconnected from humanity, accountants are vitally connected to other human beings. And I'd hazard to guess that most people who work in a bureaucracy are painfully aware of the evidence put forward by generations of historians that the horror of Hitler's Germany could never have taken place without the blind eye of most of the German bureaucratic state. If you become an accountant or a bureaucrat, it does not mean you lose your humanity and turn into something else. I would also argue that "compartmentalization" was an enormous part of how the German nation was led into barbarism, as bureaucrats could go home and sleep at night thinking, "I'm not persecuting Jews. I'm just making sure they get on the trains to go to their camps."

In the chapter titled "The Arrow of History," Harari starts to envision how one might create this all-encompassing world order:

> Merchants, conquerors, and prophets were the first people who managed to transcend the binary evolutionary division, 'us vs them,' and to foresee the potential unity of humankind. For the merchants, the entire world was a single market, and all humans were potential customers. They tried to establish an economic order that would apply to all, everywhere. For the conquerors, the entire world was a single empire, and all humans were potential subjects. And for the prophets, the entire world held a single truth, and all humans were potential believers.[13]

One might almost imagine Harari working in his academic ivory tower pondering, "What did history's most dangerous megalomaniacs do right, and how can my friends avoid their mistakes?"

In the chapter that follows, "The Scent of Money," Harari seems to have found his answer. The tyrants of the past just didn't bribe enough people, and when that didn't work, they needed to be more brutal. Harari sums up the problem in the concluding paragraph of his chapter:

> It is common nowadays to believe that the market always prevails, and that the dams erected by kings, priests, and communities cannot hold back the tides of money. This is naive. Brutal warriors, religious fanatics, and concerned citizens have repeatedly managed to trounce calculating merchants, and even to reshape the economy. It is therefore impossible to understand the unification of humankind as a purely economic process. In order to understand how thousands of isolated cultures coalesced over time to form the global village of today, we must take into account the role of gold and silver, but we cannot disregard the equally crucial role of steel.[14]

That paragraph deeply troubles me. It seems to suggest that the success of any political system is based on the use of force, rather than persuasion. And rather than the persuasion that typifies political discourse in a republic, Harari seems to prefer the force used by an empire.

If you are a Star Wars fan, or even just a casual reader of history, you might be appalled to learn that Harari LOVES empires. He seeks to glorify them, despite how much brutality they may have caused to their people and others they deemed inferior. In a section titled "Evil Empires?" he lays out his belief:

> The truth is that empire has been the world's most common form of political organization for the last 2,500 years. Most humans during these two and a half millennia have lived in empires. Empire is also a very stable form of government. Most empires have found it alarmingly easy to put down rebellions. In general, they have been toppled only by external invasion or by a split within the ruling elite. Conversely, conquered peoples don't have a very good record of freeing themselves from their imperial

overlords. Most have remained subjugated for hundreds of years. Typically, they have been slowly digested by the conquering empire, until their distinct cultures fizzled out.[15]

This is pretty much the standard left-wing critique of Western civilization, and yet Harari is saying that the obliteration of native cultures was a good thing. I stand second to none in the defense of Western values as developed during the Enlightenment.

But I am not so blind as to deny the horrible historical acts perpetrated by Europeans as they spread across the globe. I will argue that these acts were a direct betrayal of the principles of the Enlightenment and should be condemned by all people. True power comes from the persuasion of rational arguments, not the sword. Harari continues with his worship of empires:

> It is tempting to divide history into good guys and bad guys, with all empires being among the bad guys. For the vast majority of empires were founded on blood, and maintained their power through oppression and war. Yet most of today's cultures are based on imperial legacies. If empires are by definition bad, what does that say about us?[16]

How can there be the slightest bit of doubt as to the methods Harari and his globalist friends will use to bring about their utopia?

They are not horrified by oppression and war.

They see oppression and war as useful tools.

And they must be used ruthlessly.

\* \* \*

Harari continues his terror parade, hyping the threat of nuclear war and climate change, scaring you into thinking you need somebody to save you, before letting you know he has the answers. [Hint, they involve genetic engineering, turning you into a robot, and creating an AI (artificial intelligence) god to rule over humanity.] I wish I were kidding. Harari begins his argument:

> An even greater challenge is posed by new technologies such as bioengineering and artificial intelligence. As we shall see in the last chapter, these technologies could be used to re-engineer not just our weapons and vehicles, but even our bodies and minds. Indeed, they could be used to create completely new types of life forms, and change the future course of evolution. Who will decide what to do with such divine powers of creation?[17]

Do these globalists now appear to you as the ultimate mad scientists? Not only will they enslave you, but they will gleefully reengineer you, perhaps with machines or gene editing to better suit their purposes.

After denigrating the "pursuit of happiness" in the American Declaration of Independence, he justifies his draconian imperial measures in one of his concluding chapters titled "And They Lived Happily Ever After."

Harari notes the amazing progress of humanity over the past five hundred years (which amazingly coincides with the development of the ideas of personal freedom as defined by the Enlightenment) and then questions whether this progress has made us happier. He writes:

> What would happen if serious research were to disprove these hypotheses? If economic growth and self-reliance do not make people happier, then what's the benefit of capitalism? What if it turns out that the subjects of large empires are generally happier than the citizens of independent states and that, for example, Ghanaians were happier under British colonial rule than under their own homegrown dictators? What would that say about the process of decolonization and the value of national self-determination?[18]

It's in a passage like this in which we come to understand how willing Harari is to engage in duplicity. In an earlier section of the book, he claimed that happiness was such an elusive concept to define that the best we could hope to do was measure pleasure. Yet now he's claiming this brave new world he wants to create will be a happier one, as our material advancement has not made us happier. Harari explains:

> This raises the possibility that the immense improvement in material conditions over the last two centuries was offset by the collapse of the family and the community. If so, the average person might well be no happier today than in 1800. Even the freedom we value so highly may be working against us. We can choose our spouses, friends, and neighbors, but they can choose to leave us. With the individual wielding unprecedented power to decide her own path in life, we find it even harder to make commitments. We thus live in an increasingly lonely world of unravelling communities and families.[19]

It's difficult to wrap one's mind around the idea that Harari and his fellow globalists are actively calling for your freedom to be restricted, just as in the terrifying dystopian future of *A Handmaid's Tale*. They claim that you can't be trusted with freedom. Freedom makes you weak and unhappy.

But Harari then moves to how he's going to make you happier. No surprise that it's by convincing you that you want what he wants. Here's the simplistic explanation put forth by Harari. Get ready for the harness to be placed around your neck:

> But the most important finding of all is that happiness does not really depend on objective conditions of either wealth, health, or even community. Rather, it depends on the correlation between objective conditions and subjective expectations. If you want a bullock-cart and get a bullock-cart, you are content. If you want

a brand-new Ferrari and get only a second-hand Fiat you feel deprived. This is why winning the lottery has, over time, the same impact on people's happiness as a debilitating car accident. When things improve, expectations balloon, and consequently even dramatic improvements in objective conditions can leave us dissatisfied.[20]

Harari is quoting a famous 1978 study titled "Lottery Winners and Accident Victims: Is Happiness Relative?" that found that lottery winners were not as happy as expected, and that accident victims who'd been rendered paraplegic, after a certain level of time had passed, reported happiness levels that were higher than expected. This was explained by the idea of expectation and habituation, and Harari's analysis is well in the mainstream of traditional thought about these findings. However, others have noted that a different interpretation is possible, even likely.

It's that our attitude, whether optimistic or pessimistic, eventually predominates, regardless of the conditions in which we live. An entire cottage industry of books has sprung up in recent years telling us that our attitude is the first thing we must fix, in order to have the best chance of achieving our desired goals. Harari even seems to flirt with this idea:

Think for a moment of your family and friends. You know some people who will remain relatively joyful, no matter what befalls them. And then there are those who are always disgruntled, no matter what gifts the world lays at their feet. We tend to believe that if we could just change our workplace, get married, finish writing that novel, buy a new car or repay the mortgage, we would be on top of the world. Yet when we get what we desire we don't seem to be any happier. Buying cars and writing novels do not change our biochemistry. They can startle it for a fleeting moment, but it is soon back to its set point.[21]

And so we come to Harari's answer to the question of human happiness. It's not your attitude, or anything you might develop on your own. It's your biochemistry. Don't worry about eating healthy food, exercising, having positive social relationships, or developing a relationship with God.

Harari is going to make it all better by giving you a happiness pill.

It'll be just like smoking pot when you were a teenager because that's how you dealt with things or drinking alcohol at ten in the morning. But somehow alcohol and other drugs never confronted the real problems of your life. Remember, it's always important to be a victim in Harari's world, not somebody who takes responsibility. Harari seems to take particular delight in the possibility of a drugged-out world, as he expresses his enthusiasm for the future depicted by Aldous Huxley in his 1932 science fiction novel, *Brave New World*:

> In Aldous Huxley's dystopian novel *Brave New World*, published in 1932 at the height of the Great Depression, happiness is the supreme value and psychiatric drugs replace the police and the ballot as the foundation of politics. Every day, each person takes a dose of 'soma,' a synthetic drug which makes people happy without harming their productivity and efficiency. The World State that governs the entire globe is never threatened by wars, revolutions, strikes or demonstrations, because all people are supremely content with their current conditions, whatever they may be. Huxley's vision is far more troubling than George Orwell's *Nineteen Eighty-Four*. Huxley's world seems monstrous to most readers, but it's hard to explain why. Everybody is happy all the time—what could be wrong with that?[22]

Actually, it's not hard to explain why Huxley's world seems monstrous to most readers. It's because it is monstrous. Most people don't want to live their life in a drugged-out haze. They want to be alive, not impaired.

They want to feel the highs and lows of life.

That's what gives life meaning.

Harari reminds me of nothing more than some religion-obsessed monk of the Middle Ages who, while seeking the enlightenment of the spiritual world, will engage in the greatest acts of brutality in the physical world. He would beat a person for an impure thought, while not realizing the damage he is doing to God's creation. He is the villain who believes himself to be the hero as he initiates the Inquisition. Harari tires not just of humanity, but indeed, he is done with the natural world itself:

> Today, the 4-billion-year-old regime of natural selection is facing a completely different challenge. In laboratories around the world, scientists are engineering living beings. They break the laws of natural selection with impunity, unbridled by even an organism's original characteristics. Eduardo Kac, a Brazilian bio-artist, decided in 2000 to create a new work of art: a fluorescent green rabbit. Kac contacted a French laboratory and offered it a fee to engineer a radiant bunny, according to his specifications. The French scientists took a run-of-the-mill rabbit embryo, implanted in its DNA a gene taken from a green, fluorescent jellyfish, and *voilà!* One green, fluorescent rabbit for *le monsieur*. Kac named the rabbit Alba.[23]

Harari is thrilled beyond belief at this turn of events, greeting it with the reverence a UFO enthusiast might react to a flying saucer landing on the south lawn of the White House. For these globalists, every scientific advance heralded the dawn of an exciting new era in which they will finally be triumphant:

> After 4 billion years of natural selection, Alba stands at the dawn of a new cosmic era, in which life will be ruled by intelligent design. If this happens, the whole of human history up to that point might, with hindsight, be reinterpreted as a process of experimentation and apprenticeship that revolutionized the game

of life. Such a process should be understood from a cosmic perspective of billions of years, rather than from a human perspective
of millennia.[24]

It's difficult to get giddier than Harari does in that passage. I'm just a
little surprised how anybody can claim Harari is an academic historian
when he uses phrases like "new cosmic era" with a straight face. Isn't
his work a little more appropriate for some New Age self-help book
than a university campus? However, Harari isn't going to be satisfied
with you feeling better about yourself, of having a clean aura like your
typical New Age zealot. You get to be biologically reengineered. Harari
explains:

> At the time of writing, the replacement of natural selection by
> intelligent design could happen in any of three ways: through
> biological engineering, cyborg engineering (cyborgs are beings
> that combine organic with non-organic parts) or the engineering
> of inorganic life.[25]

If by chance you find yourself a little concerned by this radical new
idea of biological engineering, Harari is quick to remind you that you
don't need to worry. In fact, you didn't even have to fear the old type
of biological engineering:

> There is nothing new about biological engineering per se. People
> have been using it for millennia in order to reshape themselves
> and other organisms. A simple example is castration. Humans
> have been castrating bulls for perhaps 10,000 years in order to
> create oxen. Oxen are less aggressive and are thus easier to train
> to pull ploughs. Humans also castrated their own young males to
> create soprano singers with enchanting voices and eunuchs who
> could safely be entrusted with overseeing the sultan's harem.[26]

Many are worried about losing their First and Second Amendment rights in this New World Order being promoted by Klaus Schwab and his globalists. But perhaps the men of the Old World Order should be equally fearful of losing their balls if Schwab and his minions develop an ear for "enchanting voices" or decide that harems are a pretty good idea.

And how far might this biological engineering go? After talking about how pigs can be genetically altered to turn bad omega-6 fatty acid into the healthier omega-3 fatty acid, Harari lets you know the full extent of his plan:

> The next generation of genetic engineering will make pigs with good fat look like child's play. Geneticists have managed not merely to extend the average life expectancy of worms, but also to engineer genius mice that display much improved memory and learning skills. Voles are small, stout rodents, resembling mice, and most varieties of moles are promiscuous. But there is one species in which boy and girl voles form long lasting and monogamous relationships. Geneticists claim to have isolated the genes responsible for vole monogamy. If the addition of a gene can turn a vole Don Juan into a loyal and loving husband, are we far off from being able to genetically engineer not only the individual abilities of rodents (and humans), but also their social structure?[27]

Let's imagine the future that Harari imagines comes to pass, and we develop remarkable technologies to cure disease or increase our abilities. Maybe people will eventually be able to do marathons in their nineties in addition to doing work that fulfills them, as they offer an unprecedented wisdom to the young. Do you imagine you will be in control of such decisions, or will you be under the thumb of the globalists, those people who think empires and a drugged-out populace are such a good idea?

But perhaps, like the globalists, you are somewhat disgusted by the physical world. You lust after the sleekness of machines. You may want to become a cyborg, like Arnold Schwarzenegger in the *Terminator* movies, or the Borg of *Star Trek*, or the dead policeman brought back to life and fitted with the latest technology to become *Robocop* in the series of movies that depict a dystopian future where police work is outsourced to an evil corporation that oppresses the citizens. Harari is happy to upgrade you:

> There is another new technology which could change the laws of life: cyborg engineering. Cyborgs are beings that combine organic and inorganic parts, such as a human with bionic hands. In a sense, nearly all of us are bionic these days, since our natural senses and functions are supplemented by devices such as eyeglasses, pacemakers, orthotics, and even computers and mobile phones (which relieve our brains of some of their data storage and processing burdens). We stand poised on the brink of becoming true cyborgs, of having inorganic features that are inseparable from our bodies, features that modify our abilities, desires, personalities, and identities.[28]

The enormous leaps of logic made by Harari are breathtaking. I'm sure you didn't realize those reading glasses made you a cyborg. Apparently, there's not much difference between the typical drugstore reading glasses you pick up for ten bucks and having a chip implanted in your head. Of course, it starts with bugs, but we know it won't end there:

> The Defense Advanced Research Projects Agency (DARPA), a US military research agency, is developing cyborgs out of insects. The idea is to implant electronic chips, detectors, and processors in the body of a fly or cockroach, which will enable either a human or an automatic operator to control the insect's movements remotely and to absorb and transmit information. Such a fly could be sitting on the wall at enemy headquarters, eavesdrop on the most secret conversations, and if it isn't caught first by a spider, could inform us exactly what the enemy was planning.[29]

When you read Harari, you sometimes feel like you're the fictional British spy Austin Powers, listening in on the plans of Dr. Evil. But instead of "sharks with frickin' lasers on their heads," you get remote control flies with chips in their bodies.

And have no fear, the cyborgs will eventually be turned on those who do not submit. You will be assimilated!

\* \* \*

But Harari seems most thrilled by the possibility of nonbiological life as the solution to those troublesome human beings who can be so difficult to organize into an army that can then be ordered to bayonet people the government doesn't like.

But even then, the army might not follow your orders unless you convince them the people they're going to bayonet are really bad people. Like those who might claim the votes need to be recounted in an election. We all know that asking for validation of a vote is the same thing as inciting an insurrection. Harari explains how we might get rid of human beings entirely:

> The third way to change the laws of life is to engineer completely inorganic beings. The most obvious examples are computer programs that can undergo independent evolution.
>
> Recent advances in machine learning already enable present-day computer programs to evolve by themselves. Though the program is initially coded by human engineers, it can subsequently acquire new information on its own, teach itself new skills, and gain insights that go beyond those of its human creators. The computer program is therefore free to evolve in directions its makers could never have envisaged.[30]

Harari sounds like such a proud parent, doesn't he? It's like he gave birth to a computer program. And if the machine starts to misbehave, well, unlike a human being, you can just turn it off. What if your laptop could also be your brain?

> Imagine another possibility—suppose you could back up your brain to a portable hard drive and then run it on your laptop. Would your laptop be able to think and feel just like a Sapiens? If so, would it be you, or someone else? What if computer programmers could create an entirely new but digital mind, composed of computer code, complete with a sense of self, consciousness, and memory? If you ran the program on your computer, would it be a person? If you deleted it, could you be charged with murder?[31]

If you believe Harari is going to simply stop with intelligent machines, you are sorely mistaken. He believes these intelligent machines will eventually take over, an event he and many others call the "singularity." In case you were having a little trouble working up the intellectual energy to consider his plans for the suicide of the human race, he helpfully highlights his genocidal plans in a section titled "The Singularity." From that section:

> Most science fiction plots describe a world in which Sapiens— identical to us—enjoy superior technology such as light-speed spaceships and laser guns. The ethical and political dilemmas central to these plots are taken from our own world, and they merely recreate our emotional and social tensions against a futuristic backdrop. Yet the real potential of future technologies is to change *Homo Sapiens* itself, including our emotions and desires, and not merely our vehicles and weapons. What is a spaceship compared to an eternally young cyborg who does not breed and has no sexuality, who can share thoughts directly with other beings, whose abilities to focus and remember are a thousand times greater than our own, and who is never angry or sad, but has emotions and desires that we cannot begin to imagine?[32]

Do you think this is a future that could ever win wide acceptance among the general public? Harari hopes you do not breed, never have sex, and instead "share thoughts directly with other beings" and that you will never be "angry or sad" and have "emotions and desires that we cannot begin to imagine."

Does this sound like any human future of which you want to be a part?

Again, Harari reminds me of a crazed religious zealot, so disgusted by the flesh that he only wants to exist in the spiritual world. But because Harari recognizes no god or spiritual plane of existence, he tries to fill the god-shaped hole in his soul with technology.

However, for those of us who do acknowledge a spiritual reality, this is an old and familiar tale. It is the common story of one who does not acknowledge the creator and, in doing so, seeks to supplant Him. In the religious traditions of the world, those who walk this path risk becoming demons and devils, the most hideous creatures in all creation.

In the afterword, "The Animal Who Became a God," he proudly declares his heresy:

> Seventy thousand years ago, *Homo Sapiens* was still an insignif-
> icant animal minding its own business in a corner of Africa. In
> the following millennia it transformed itself into the master of the
> entire planet and the terror of the ecosystem. Today it stands on
> the verge of becoming a god, poised to acquire not only eternal
> youth, but also the divine abilities of creation and destruction.[33]

We know the type of future Harari envisions for human beings: genetic manipulation, robotic enhancements, and nonorganic life that eventually rules over us.

But we know who the real rulers will be.

The globalists, with Klaus Schwab, or his downloaded brain, giving us all orders from his laptop.

* * *

In his next book, *Homo Deus: A Brief History of Tomorrow*, Harari provides more details on his preferred future. Part 1 is titled "Homo Sapiens Conquers the World," and Part 2 is "Homo Sapiens Gives Meaning to the World," essentially a recap of many of the points he made in *Sapiens*.

Part 3, "Homo Sapiens Loses Control," is where Harari really gets going with his futuristic plans, in a chapter titled "The Time Bomb in the Laboratory." (Now, you might be forgiven if you thought the chapter was about China and the United States experimenting with dangerous bat viruses and how one escaped, causing a worldwide pandemic and killing millions, but you'd be mistaken.) Instead, this is what Harari had to say:

> In 2016 the world is dominated by the liberal package of individualism, human rights, democracy, and the free market. Yet twenty-first century science is undermining the foundations of the liberal order. Because science does not deal with questions of value, it cannot determine whether liberals are right in valuing liberty more than equality, or in valuing the individual more than the collective. However, like every other religion, liberalism too is based not only on abstract ethical judgments, but also on what it believes to be factual statements. And these factual statements just don't stand up to rigorous scientific scrutiny.[34]

In Harari's vision, if you like individualism, human rights, democracy, and the free market, you're just a deluded fool. It's all part of some "imagined order" rather than a system developed by brilliant, compassionate people over the centuries as the most effective way for us to live together in a manner that is conducive to the greatest good for the largest number of people. If you don't believe Harari is interested in tearing down all these pillars of a civil society, I offer this passage:

> To the best of our scientific understanding, determinism and randomness have divided the entire cake between them, leaving not even a crumb for 'freedom.' The sacred word 'freedom' turns out to be, just like 'soul,' a hollow term empty of any discernible meaning. Free will exists only in the imaginary stories we humans have invented.[35]

It staggers the mind that the person who wrote those words is not universally condemned by all the supposed lovers of freedom. One almost imagines they're reading the words of a young Adolph Hitler or Joseph Stalin, rather than the writings of an Israeli academic. If there's no such thing as free will, how could anybody ever be prosecuted for rape, murder, or any crime? This is a version of hell where nothing is forbidden, and all things are permitted.

After attacking liberalism all through the chapter, even equating medieval crusaders and today's liberals as similarly delusional, Harari lays it out:

> However, once the heretical scientific insights are translated into everyday technology, routine activities and economic structures, it will become increasingly difficult to sustain this double-game [believing in science and free will]—and we—or our heirs—will probably require a brand-new package of religious beliefs and political institutions. At the beginning of the third millennium liberalism is threatened not by the idea that 'there are no free individuals,' but rather by concrete technologies. We are about to face a flood of extremely useful devices, tools and structures that make no allowance for the free will of individual humans. Will democracy, the free market and human rights survive this flood?[36]

It's genuinely comical to read how people like Harari believe that technological changes will bring about these massive changes to society. These same arguments were being made by Zbigniew Brzezinski in the 1970s.

The World War II order is breaking down!

Highways now link one side of the country to another!

People can pick up the phone on the West Coast and immediately talk to somebody on the East Coast!

We have planes that can take your family to Europe in just a few hours!

You can heat your dinner in just a few minutes in a microwave oven!

Sadly, none of these technological marvels created the breathtaking changes the globalists thought they would provoke.

In his chapter titled "The Great Decoupling," this is what Harari predicts for the twenty-first century:

1. Humans will lose their economic and military usefulness; hence the economic and political system will stop attaching much value to them.
2. The system will continue to find value in humans collectively, but not in unique individuals.
3. The system will still find value in some unique individuals, but these will constitute a new elite of upgraded superhumans rather than the mass of the population.[37]

You can't say that Harari doesn't have big plans. It's just that they're insane, the ravings of a dictator-in-training. One wonders how he might retain the simplest of human relations. Does he tell his significant other he has no free will? I wonder how his partner feels, though, about the whole, eternally young cyborg, sexless, and nonbreeding plan?

That must have prompted at least a few discussions in their relationship.

If you have been curious as to what people mean when they talk about "transhumanism," this is your answer. You will be a biological organism with machine upgrades, and those upgrades will come at the cost of stripping you of what is the most human thing about you.

After writing several pages showing how humans will be less valuable to the "system" in the years to come, and governments will care less about them, Harari documents what he sees as the final threat to liberalism:

> The third threat to liberalism is that some people will remain both indispensable and undecipherable, but they will constitute a small and privileged elite of upgraded humans. These superhumans will enjoy unheard-of abilities and unprecedented creativity which will allow them to go on making many of the most important decisions in the world. They will perform crucial services for the system, while the system could neither understand or manage them. However, most humans will not be upgraded, and will consequently become an inferior caste dominated by both computer algorithms and the new superhumans.[38]

I'm genuinely trying to resist making Nazi comparisons in this book. But it's so difficult when these globalists start using expressions like "new superhumans."

Harari is enamored of the idea that some people will rule, and others will become part of an "inferior caste." It's not too much of a leap to wonder if the globalists might decide at some point that this inferior caste no longer warrants continued survival and needs to be liquidated.

Harari's messianic fervor appears to recognize no bounds. When people scoff at claims that these globalists are setting up a new religion, they might want to read what they say in their books:

> The new religions are unlikely to emerge from the caves of Afghanistan or from the madrassas of the Middle East. Rather, they will emerge from research laboratories. Just as socialism took over the world by promising salvation through steam and electricity, so in the coming decades new techno-religions may conquer the world by promising salvation through algorithms and genes.

Despite all the talk of radical Islam or Christian fundamentalism, the most interesting place in the world from a religious perspective is not the Islamic State or the Bible Belt, but Silicon Valley. That's where hi-tech gurus are brewing for us brave new religions that have little to do with God, and everything to do with technology.[39]

What does a person do when they realize that all the crazy claims made about these globalists are pretty close to the truth? These globalists do want to dethrone God from his throne in heaven and place themselves in charge.

That's not hyperbole, but straight from their own writings.

At the end of *Homo Deus*, Harari provides his three main points:

1. Science is converging on an all-encompassing dogma, which says that organisms are algorithms and life is data processing.
2. Intelligence is decoupling from consciousness.
3. Non-conscious, but highly intelligent algorithms may soon know us better than we know ourselves.[40]

*Homo Deus* literally means "man is God." That is what the globalists are pushing. If there is one thing that religion has done, it is to cause people to consider things outside of themselves. It is religion that caused people to worry about feeding the poor, educating the young, removing people from slavery, and making sure that all enjoy equal opportunity. At its best, religion breaks down walls, requiring people to see others as fellow children of God, all equally valuable.

By agreeing that all people have value, there can be no impulse to harm or rid ourselves of them. The more people embrace equality and freedom, the closer they are to God's natural order. When one understands the philosophical underpinnings of a belief in God, it becomes clear that these globalists are nothing less than an opposition force to that belief.

What else would you call an opposition force to God other than devils and demons?

\* \* \*

The third book in Harari's trilogy is titled *21 Lessons for the 21st Century*, published in 2018, which has as its first endorser Bill Gates, who wrote, "I'm a big fan of everything Harari has written, and his latest is no exception."

One wonders, if Harari has written everything he thinks is important about humanity's past in *Sapiens*, and covered our future in *Homo Deus*, what could there possibly be left to say?

I consider *21 Lessons for the 21st Century* to be something genuinely different from his two earlier books. Has Harari developed a conscience? Is he backing away from the globalists? There is some evidence for this belief.

I don't plan to go through all twenty-one lessons but will simply hit a few of the more disturbing highlights. As he often does, Harari starts out sounding rational, as in this passage:

> Truth and power can travel together only so far. Sooner or later, they go their separate paths. If you want power, at some point you will have to spread fiction. If you want to know the truth about the world, at some point you will have to renounce power. You will have to admit things—for example, about the source of your power—that will anger allies, dishearten followers, or undermine social harmony. Scholars throughout history have faced this dilemma: do they serve power or truth? Should they aim to unite people by making everyone believe the same story, or should they let people know the truth even at the price of disunity?[41]

I find it difficult to find any fault with that statement. That's been my experience on several occasions. Telling the truth often gets me less power. However, I must point to the fact that some of the most popular figures today with the largest audiences, such as me, Joe Rogan, Jordan Peterson, and Tucker Carlson, are relentless truth-tellers. In retrospect, I must disagree with Harari that telling the truth will forever bar you from the halls of power. It just might take the public a little longer to catch up.

But the power obtained by telling the truth is more lasting than the power obtained by telling lies.

It's difficult to reconcile this passage about truth and power with how, in his previous books, Harari has enthusiastically endorsed the desirability of empires, the stripping away of civil rights from people, and the creation of a caste system of superhumans and the non-superhumans who will be ruled by algorithms and genetic engineering.

And Harari seems to take great delight in his claim that even Disney is joining him in his attack on free will:

> Disney has built its empire by retelling one myth over and over. In countless Disney movies, the heroes face difficulties and dangers, but they eventually triumph by finding their authentic self and following their free choices. *Inside Out* brutally dismantles this myth. It adopts the latest neurobiological view of humans and takes viewers on a journey into Riley's brain only to discover that she has no authentic self and that she never makes any free choices. Riley is in fact a huge robot managed by a collection of conflicting biochemical mechanisms, which the movie personifies as cute cartoon characters: the yellow and cheerful Joy, the blue and morose Sadness, the red and short-tempered Anger, and so on . . .
>
> . . . The truly amazing thing is not only that Disney dared to market a movie with such a radical message but that it became a worldwide hit. Perhaps it succeeded so well because *Inside Out* is a comedy with a happy ending, and most viewers could have missed both its neurological meaning and its sinister implications.[42]

Does it seem odd to you that an academic is spending so much time dissecting the plot of a Disney children's movie? It doesn't to me because stories, especially those told to children, are vitally important to the future of a society. As Disney finds themselves under increasing attack by parents in 2022 for what they view as attempts to break up the traditional family, it's interesting to note Harari saw this pattern emerging as early as 2015. What other crimes can be perpetrated against children when you teach them they are not responsible for their actions and should avoid those who try to teach them they are responsible?

From Disney's *Inside Out* Harari pivots back to Aldous Huxley's *Brave New World*, a book that Harari believes should serve as a blueprint for our world:

> In this brave new world, the World Government uses advanced biotechnology and social engineering to make sure that everyone is always content, and no one has any reason to rebel. It is as if Joy, Sadness, and the other characters in Riley's brain have been turned into loyal government agents. There is therefore no need for a secret police, concentration camps, or a Ministry of Love a la Orwell's 1984. Indeed, Huxley's genius consists in showing that you can control people far more securely through love and pleasure than through fear and violence.[43]

Harari admires the World Government of *Brave New World*. I think it's important for the regular reader to understand the globalists don't want to create visible incidents of violence against their opponents.

However, given what they have written, it's clear to me that their ideology would have no trouble with committing acts of violence in ways that are not visible to the public.

But then Harari seemed to take a detour, making me wonder what has changed in his thinking.

The last section of the book is an admirable defense of trying to discover the truth about things. And yet he also expresses a fear that such explorations may not exist in the near future:

As technology improved, two things happened. First, as the flint knives gradually evolved into nuclear missiles, destabilizing the social order became more dangerous. Second, as cave paintings gradually evolved into television broadcasts, it became easier to delude people. In the future, algorithms might bring this process to completion, making it well-nigh impossible for people to observe the reality about themselves. It will be the algorithms that will decide for us who we are and what we should know about ourselves.

For a few more years or decades, we still have a choice. If we make the effort, we can still investigate who we really are. But if we want to make use of this opportunity, we had better do it now.[44]

When I read this last passage I detected a lament, the passing of a world of which Harari was immensely fond.

As a Christian, I'm always willing to accept a sinner who has seen the error of his ways. It's one of the superpowers of being a Christian. We rejoice over the reconciliation of the greatest sinner even more than the enduring faithfulness of the regular believer.

After the conclusion of *21 Lessons for the 21st Century*, there is a long interview with Harari, which gives me even more support for this belief. If the individual is as unimportant as Harari has been saying in his previous books, why is it that he feels the need to share so much about himself? Here are some selections:

> In the twenty-first century the price we pay for ignorance about ourselves will increase dramatically, because governments and corporations are now gaining unprecedented abilities to hack and manipulate human choice. And the easiest people to manipulate are those who believe in free will—because they refuse to acknowledge that they can be manipulated.[45]

I don't agree with Harari about the lack of genuine free will in people, but I do agree that there is a great deal of manipulation in today's media environment. In fact, in this interview Harari does acknowledge that there can be free will, but says that much of what we do is not because of free will, but because of media manipulation. However, our disagreements are likely to be a matter of degree, rather than wholesale opposition.

Again, when Harari discusses the negative aspects of Silicon Valley, I agree with much of what he says and find our disagreement lies in what we believe is genuinely on the mind of those in charge in Silicon Valley. But determining the motives of individuals is fraught with uncertainty. We do our best, based on the rational interpretation of their words. I'm comfortable saying both Harari and I are guessing as to their true intentions, but it's the best we can do. This is Harari's answer to the question of whether the leaders of Silicon Valley are evil:

> My impression is that though Silicon Valley leaders may well be naïve and sometimes disingenuous, they are seldom evil. They genuinely believe that their corporations benefit humanity. But they are often unaware, or uninterested, in the broader economic, social, and political consequences of their actions. Part of the problem is that Silicon Valley is led by genius engineers who know mathematics and computer science very well but can be quite naïve when it comes to history, philosophy, and politics. This is why historians, philosophers, and social critics have a particularly important role to play.[46]

Perhaps I am reading too much into Harari's comments, but it seems as if he has developed an appreciation of the shortcoming of his Big Tech gods. They are not the fountain of all worthwhile wisdom. I find Harari coming dangerously close to believing that since none can be fully trusted, the best we can do is let all have a voice in their future and, to the maximum extent possible with a functioning society, allow people to have their freedom.

In answer to the question about what love means for him, Harari provided a deeply emotional response:

> Love is being connected. To love means to be liberated from the obsession with whatever thoughts, emotions, and desires pop into my own mind right now, and instead listen to others and see what is happening with them. It starts with simple things, such as listening to somebody else. When you talk with someone and you care mainly about what you want to say, you can't really hear that person. You are just waiting for the moment he or she stops talking, so you can finally get a word in. But when you let go of your own thoughts, you can listen.[47]

I am genuinely puzzled that the same person who wrote of a future in which the ideal human would be an "eternally young cyborg," sexless and nonbreeding, could have such sentiments.

This book is based on the premise that the globalists believe they know better than the average person how to run their lives. Because they consider themselves to be of a superior caste of human beings, they do not see the value of talking with us. It is said that the opposite of love is not hate, but indifference. The globalists seem supremely indifferent to the human beings in whose name they are supposedly making their plans.

I fail to understand how the writer who wrote so dispassionately of the castration of young boys for their singing voices or to create a class of eunuchs to guard a sultan's harem can express such tenderness in his personal relationships.

I began this chapter characterizing Harari as a "Robocop for the Empire," a creature of flesh and metal who serves a corrupt and dictatorial corporate government. And I believe I have provided abundant evidence to justify this characterization.

However, a Christian also believes that each saint has a past and every sinner a future. That is why we pray for our enemies and are eternally vigilant for the earliest sign of a turn away from evil, and toward goodness.

As much as I believe Harari is currently acting as a "Robocop for the Empire" that Klaus Schwab and the globalists wish to establish, I see signs of his humanity emerging and his conscience troubling him.

The greatest victory is not to destroy your enemy, but to welcome him back when he realizes the error of his ways.

I do not believe the final word has been written as to whether Yuval Noah Harari is a force for evil or good in this world.

I will live in the hope that he finds his way back to the light.

However, the choice is for him to decide. Unlike the globalists, God does not force you to do anything. One must come to their decisions voluntarily and without coercion if they are to have any meaning at all.

Making voluntary decisions is one of the most important aspects of living as a free human being and emerging as one who is calm and at peace with the world.

*Chapter Six*

# You Probably Won't Face a Firing Squad in the Great Reset, but You May Be Put in a Digital Gulag

We've spent a lot of time reviewing the writings of Klaus Schwab and other globalists, but what is the evidence these plans are being put into motion?

I think it's important to realize we're unlikely to find an email from Klaus Schwab directing some world leader, like say Justin Trudeau of Canada, on how to deal with a situation. However, when we understand the philosophy of the globalists, the question is can we find examples that appear consistent enough with their views that we can assume their involvement at some level?

I believe we can find multiple examples of such efforts, beginning first with the trucker convoy that surrounded the Canadian Parliament in January and February of 2022 in protest of COVID restrictions. This is how the protests were described in *Fortune* magazine:

> The brigade of truck-driving protestors from Canada first converged in Ottawa on Jan. 28, occupying various streets around the nation's capital. The protest began in opposition to the

introduction of a mandate requiring all cross-border truck drivers to be vaccinated against COVID-19.

According to the Canadian Trucking Alliance, roughly 90% of Canadian truck drivers were already vaccinated, but a minority of truckers objected to the new requirement for drivers hauling goods between Canada and the U.S.

As the protests and their convoy spread across Canada, the focus of the demonstration expanded to oppose all pandemic-era mandates, such as mask requirements and COVID vaccine passport check-ins.[1]

You might have followed the trucker protests in Canada, but maybe you didn't. I thought the *Fortune* article did a pretty good job of summarizing how the protest started. Most protest movements start with a single issue, such as in the United States with the death of George Floyd in police custody, and then develop into discussion of some larger issues, such as police practices across the country and their effect on communities of color.

Democracies are born in protest, and it is what gives them vitality. As we have abundantly shown in this book, the globalists are not fond of protests, as they believe there is no reason to talk with their opponents. Did Trudeau deal with the protestors in a way consistent with a globalist approach? You decide:

For protestors, the first bad omen for their movement hit on Feb. 5 when GoFundMe suspended Lich's fundraising account after receiving police reports of protest violence and other unlawful activity.

"This fundraiser is now in violation of our Terms of Service (Term 8, which prohibits the promotion of violence or harassment) and has been removed from the platform," GoFundMe said, adding that it would return the $8 million raised back to donors.

Undeterred by the loss of millions, protest organizers simply switched fundraising tactics. Shortly after GoFundMe shut down the group's main account, four protest supporters, calling themselves HonkHonkHodl, launched a new fundraising page on crypto fundraising site, Tallycoin.[2]

The article continues by informing the readers that the crypto site was then shut down by Canada's federal police, and transactions of thirty-four crypto wallets were to be halted. Eventually, another 146 crypto wallets were also frozen.[3] The government of Canada had, without due process, restricted the financial transactions of law-abiding Canadians. A dangerous precedent had just been set by the Trudeau government. But they weren't finished:

> Last Monday, Canada's Prime Minister Justin Trudeau delivered the Freedom Convoy campaign its final death blow and invoked the Emergencies Act for the first time in Canadian history, empowering police to move against the protestors.
>
> "We cannot and will not allow illegal and dangerous activities to continue," Trudeau said as he invoked the Emergencies Act, which granted police greater leeway to impose fines, imprison protestors, and tow vehicles blocking roads . . .
>
> The Emergencies Act also compelled financial institutions to comply with police orders to freeze funds associated with "designated persons"—in this case, protestors. With funds hobbled, public sentiment turning against them, and the threat of arrest and financial sanctions looming, the protest movement began to lose momentum.[4]

For most of my life, I've considered Canada to have almost the same values as the United States. And yet, what Trudeau did to the truckers is appalling, something one would expect to see in some third-world dictatorship.

Can you imagine an American president doing something similar to the anti-war or civil rights protests of the 1960s? To the anti-nuclear protests of the 1980s? To the Black Lives Matter protests/riots of 2020?

Can this get any worse? Yes, it can. Because technology, which can link things together, makes it even easier for the government to shut you down if they don't like the way you're behaving.

Imagine a scenario where the Canadian government could shut off the mobile banking of every protestor at the Trucker Convoy. Not by researching who was there and contacting their banking institutions. They could simply monitor the cellular GPS of all peaceful protestors (as they did for the January 6 protestors) and turn off their mobile banking.

Now just imagine if they turned off all their mobile apps. Or, if we were all linked into a Central Bank Digital Currency, and they deducted social credits, or pulled money off their tokenized central bank digital currency. Imagine a world where your every movement is tracked. Your opinions would be analyzed by artificial intelligence (AI), and you could be instantly penalized for wrong thinking.

This is the world that the global elites would like to create with the Great Reset.

This is not fantasy.

This is not unrealistic conspiracy theory. The technology is already there, and this is the stated goal by global governments and the World Economic Forum.

In response to Putin's invasion of Ukraine, Apple Pay and Google Pay shut off the finances of countless ordinary Russian citizens. Viral photos surfaced of massive lines at Moscow's metro system showing thousands of citizens unable to access their finances, fumbling about in search of cash for train tickets. This is how it was reported in England on February 28, 2022:

> Russians can no longer use their bank cards with Google Pay and
> Apple Pay as newly imposed financial sanctions hit the country.

> "Apple Pay doesn't work in Russia. My bank sent a message saying services might not be working due to market changes," a Russian citizen told Metro.co.uk on Sunday . . .
>
> As of 2020, 29% of Russians reported using Google Pay, while 20% used Apple Pay.[5]

Going cashless means your ability to even exist in society can be simply shut off at any time by the government. Do we wonder why Russians might believe the United States is interested in ruining their country? There is a dispute between the leaders of Russia and the West around the notion that we are actively trying to harm the citizens of Russia. How is any of this allowed?

Federal Reserve chairman Jerome Powell and the Federal Reserve Bank explored a digital dollar. From a January 20, 2022, CNBC report on the effort:

> The Federal Reserve on Thursday released its long-awaited exploration of a digital dollar but took no position on the issuance of a central bank digital currency.
>
> Instead, the central bank's 40-page document explores a plethora of issues and notes that public comment will be solicited.
>
> Fed Governor Leal Brainard, who has been nominated as vice chair, is the biggest advocate for the project, while other officials have expressed skepticism . . .
>
> "We look forward to engaging with the public, elected representatives, and a broad range of stakeholders as we examine the positives and negatives of a central bank digital currency in the United States," Powell said in a statement.[6]

Now, this book takes a certain view on how globalists will execute their plans, not showing their hand, while working behind the scenes to bring it about. As I read Powell's statement, he sounds like a typical globalist, using language like "engaging with the public, elected representatives, and a broad range of stakeholders," which makes me suspect they are further along in their efforts than they admit.

China has already rolled out a pilot program for a digital currency, as detailed in a January 10, 2022, CNBC article:

> China is ramping up its efforts to roll out the digital yuan to the broader population, as the country's technology giants like Alibaba and Tencent jump on board . . .
>
> Also known as the e-CNY, it's designed to replace the cash and coins already in circulation. It is not a cryptocurrency like bitcoin, in part because it's controlled and issued by the central bank. Bitcoin is a decentralized digital currency that isn't backed by any central banks or a single administrator.
>
> China's digital yuan is a form of central bank digital currency (CBDC) which many other central banks around the world are also working on—though the Chinese central bank is way ahead of its global peers.[7]

This isn't fantasyland. It's already here, and the elites are just waiting for the right crisis or incentives to usher people into the new digital system.

As we try to make sense of the Russia/Ukraine war, it's probably useful to ask whether the president of Ukraine, Volodymyr Zelenskyy, seems to be on the side of freedom or on the side of the globalists. If we accept the idea that the globalists are attempting to seize control of technology, we might suspect Zelenskyy's motives when he announced an effort in February 2020 to put the "State in a Smartphone." This is from a Ukrainian publication:

> Ukraine's president and prime minister on February 6 presented the country's mobile e-governance application Diia (action), which aims to digitize all government services and play a central role in President Volodymr Zelensyy's "State in a Smartphone" concept . . .

> By the end of the winter, a digital passport will appear in the
> app, which will allow users to travel domestically, conduct bank-
> ing and use medical services.[8]

This "State in a Smartphone" effort was led by Mykhailo Fedorov,
the vice prime minister and minister of Digital Transformation for
Ukraine. He is also a "Young Global Leader" for the World Economic
Forum and was a panelist at the WEF "Scaling Up Digital Identity
Systems" session. This is how he is described in his biography on the
World Economic Forum:

> Mykhailo Fedorov is Vice Prime Minister and Minister of Digital
> Transformation of Ukraine. The youngest minister in the history
> of Ukrainian politics, Fedorov, at the age of 30, managed to suc-
> ceed both with opening his own businesses as well as with leading
> the country's digital revolution. His most important project as
> minister is the "State in a Smartphone" which aims, by 2024, to
> have 100% of all government services available online, with 20%
> of services provided automatically without the intervention of an
> official and one online form to receive a package of services.[9]

His biography for the WEF has stated that his most important goal is
"the State in a Smartphone," which aims by 2024 to have 100 percent
of all government services available online (seems harmless), with 20
percent of services provided automatically without intervention of an
official (seems scary). Imagine our government automatically removing money from your account. Or automatically freezing your account
based on your right to peacefully protest, your political views, or your
carbon footprint.

Fedorov said during his presentation to the World Economic
Forum in 2021:

> "Our goal is to enable all life situations with this digital ID," said
> Fedorov, adding, "The pandemic has accelerated our progress.

First of all, people are really now demanding digital, online services. People have no choice but to trust technology.

"We believe that we have to make the best product possible, a
high-quality product, a product that is so convenient that a person
will be able to disrupt their stereotypes, the breakthrough from
their fears, and start using a government-made application."[10]

Wow! You're talking about a centralized system totally controlled by
the government that not only tracks and knows everything about
you, but can freeze your account as it sees fit! Not only that, but these
Ukrainian Digital ID services will also feature vaccination, electronic
passports, and Ukrainian Covid Certificates.

Ukraine was pioneering a system that governments all around the
world could use as a template to control their populations.

If we look at the Russian invasion of Ukraine with that perspective,
do Putin's actions seem as difficult to understand?

\* \* \*

Imagine all your money is no longer money. It's a credit within a centralized digital system that is administered by the government.

It has a fully tracked and traceable serial number.

It could be coded to not allow you to buy Meat, Bitcoin, Air Travel,
or Gold.

It could block your ability to buy a pillow from Mike Lindell's
company, MyPillow.

Or it could be blocked from purchasing products from my supple-
ment store at InfoWars.

Now factor in a digital World ID, a vaccine passport that expires
if you're not updated on your boosters and is also tracking your GPS
movements to know if you've been at the wrong gatherings or protests. It can measure how far you've traveled and if you're committing
the cardinal sin of too much carbon emissions. Say, do, buy, travel, or
translate with "the wrong" company, and your credits can be taxed, or

frozen. This becomes a tool far outside of the scope of monetary policy; it becomes a digital gulag.

Of course, we've all heard of the gulags, forced labor camps maintained in the Soviet Union. These gulags become prisons used to capture, control, and enslave dissidents. And what was a dissident? Simply a person who opposed the official policy of an authoritarian state. Now imagine this digital gulag being used in countries around the world, or in the United States.

In today's world, they do not need a physical gulag or prison camp. They just need to roll out the World ID system, vaccine passports, and Central Bank Digital Currency. Once they have this, they can imprison anyone they want into a digital gulag.

Banking access cut off.

Medical access shut off.

Taxes confiscated automatically.

And "credits," which used to be "money," are 100 percent programmable to be deleted, frozen, or removed if you practice "wrong think."

Not up to date with your twelfth booster shot? Financial accounts frozen. Purchasing too much meat, or buying products from the wrong companies? Frozen! Attending a peaceful protest that the government deems troublesome? Frozen!

Sure, I was the first person in history to be totally censored and deplatformed from social media. Sure, I was the first person to have all social media, tech companies, and financial institutions remove me from their services. That was bad, but just imagine what happens when everything is centralized into a World ID, vaccine passport, and Central Bank Digital Currency.

But to make this just a little scarier, let's talk about the Chinese Social Credit Score System, which will certainly tie into your digital money. This is from a *Business Insider* article in December 2021 on the system:

> The Chinese Communist Party has been constructing a moral
> ranking system for years that will monitor the behavior of its

enormous population—and rank them all based on their "social credit"...

Like private credit scores, a person's social score can move up and down depending on their behavior.

The exact methodology is a secret—but examples of infractions include bad driving, smoking in non-smoking zones, buying too many video games, and posting fake news online, specifically about terrorist attacks or airport security.

Other potential punishable offenses include spending too long playing video games, wasting money on frivolous purchases, and posting on social media.[11]

Being discredited or blacklisted in China makes it nearly impossible to get a job, travel, buy things from stores, get a mortgage, or have children. You could also find your Internet speed slowed down or be prevented from boarding an airplane. That's not to mention the public shaming component, as there is even an application that shows you the names and photos of everyone around you who is low on social credits, or in financial debt![12]

All of this is done through algorithmic data, which allows China to monitor everything and build profiles of citizens. Today, massive surveillance cameras are not needed. Your phone is a GPS system, and everything is trackable and traceable through your Internet and financial history.

This is not me presenting a baseless conspiracy theory, as they like to say.

This is all factual and occurring in real time. Then when you combine the modern features of Big Tech, between Google, social media apps, and Big Banking, your entire life can be easily scored and programmed through a credit system. It is not difficult to see how a Central Bank Digital Currency of programmable financial credits would tie into an overall World ID, vaccine passport, and Social Credit Score system.

Now think about the fact Justin Trudeau openly stated that the government he admires most is China. This is from the *Toronto Sun* in February 2011 regarding Trudeau's deep respect for China's form of government:

> There should be no surprise Prime Minister Justin Trudeau says he needs more evidence before concluding China's horrific treatment of its minority Uyghur Muslim population is a genocide, despite having agreed two years ago that Canada's treatment of its Indigenous population was a genocide.
>
> As Maya Angelou famously put it: "When people show you who they are, believe them the first time."
>
> While Trudeau is taking a less starry-eyed view of China these days, in 2013, as Liberal leader, he was asked during a "Ladies Night" Liberal fundraiser what country he most admired besides Canada.
>
> He responded: "There's a level of admiration I actually have for China. Their basic dictatorship is actually allowing them to turn their economy around on a dime and say, 'We need to go green, we want to start investing in solar'."[13]

Think about the fact that countries all over the world are scrambling to launch digital IDs, vaccine passports, and Central Bank Digital Currencies. Global elites see this as a necessary control tool to retain total power over the population and all social behaviors.

Do you see how this all ties back to a digital wallet, which is a front for a social credit score system? The vaccine passports are the Trojan horse for a World ID, integrated with a Central Bank Digital Currency and Social Credit Score system.

The breadcrumbs are all laid out, ever so neatly in a row.

But it gets even more dystopian if you think about what happened in Canada during the Trucker Protests of 2022. Under the Emergency Act, Justin Trudeau used terrorism laws to seize the bank accounts of people who donated as little as $50.

Simply stated, they used emergency orders to suspend the rule of law, labeled them as terrorists, and seized their financial assets.

Appearing on *The Glenn Beck Program*, former PayPal executive David Sacks said, "You have all the ingredients that Justin Trudeau was able to seize on. All you're really lacking is the emergency."[14]

Glenn's conversation with Sacks begins with the following questions: "How far away from this system are we to have a true credit score? Do you see this happening sooner rather than later? And what do we do to stop it?"[15]

The former PayPal executive responded:

Well, this is my main concern is at the end of the day, I'm not a Canadian and I watch with sadness what's happening over there, but ultimately it's going to be up to Canadians to govern themselves. What I'm mostly concerned about is the precedent that Trudeau has set that progressives here in America might look to and implement. And let's identify the elements of the ingredients of this toxic stew that already exists over here.

First of all, you've got big tech companies like my Alma Mater PayPal have been freezing accounts based on working with partisan political groups to shut people out of the financial system. That practice is already taking place.

Second, you've got state of emergencies in states like California, where I live, where the governor is still operating under a state of emergency. He has invoked emergency powers that never seem to end, even though we just had a Super Bowl where 30,000 people were sitting elbow to elbow without any masks on, yet we're still in the state of emergency.

Third, we have, recently the Department of Homeland security has now defined misinformation about COVID or the election to be a contributor to the terrorist threat level.

So, in other words, misinformation in their view, can contribute to terrorism. So, we have now all the ingredients where you have politicians invoking state of emergencies, you've got big tech companies shunning people out of the political system, and you've got this very scary and dangerous redefinition of terrorism to effectively apply to domestic political descent. So you have all the ingredients there that Justin Trudeau was able to seize on.

And all you're really lacking is the emergency necessary to invoke those powers. So that is what I'm afraid of is. I see all the precedents coming together, but we have one thing in the United States that Canada doesn't have, which is a rich, constitutional tradition. We have the protections under the constitution. And so I'm hopeful that our Supreme Court would protect us against an authoritarian attack on our liberties this way. However, there are many in our political system who want to pack the Supreme Court.[16]

I know, this is some scary stuff. But the only way we can defeat this is to understand what's really happening. Believe me, I'd rather be on the beach retired somewhere.

But let's skip the vacation for now and get some context to the Canadian situation.

Barry MacKillop, deputy director of Financial Transactions and Reports Analysis Center, FINTRAC, spoke before Canada's House of Commons finance committee:

> The money the organizers managed to raise was not only not cash that funded terrorism or was in any way money laundering. It was simply a way for people living in what they thought was a democratic country believing was a safe way of expressing their position on an issue. These citizens subsequently, evidently treated by their government as potential terrorists and money launderers were in fact fed up with COVID and were upset and just wanted to support the cause.[17]

Yes, the democratic country of Canada, one in which Prime Minister Justin Trudeau said on December 2020, "Canada will always stand up for the right of peaceful protest anywhere around the world."[18]

Trudeau's statement was made while criticizing India for its police response to farmer's blockades in Delhi. So, let's unpack this: Canada openly condemned foreign governments for squashing legitimate protests. Then, when a protest in Canada threatened their political agenda, they used emergency orders to label them as potential terrorists and freeze their financial assets.

* * *

Now think about the Department of Homeland Security, which issued a bulletin from the National Terrorism Advisory System on February 7, 2022, which was plastered on all news channels, which stated on their website:

> The United States remains in a heightened threat environment fueled by several factors, including an online environment filled with false or misleading narratives and conspiracy theories, and other forms of mis-dis-and-mal-information (MDM) introduced and/or amplified by foreign and domestic threat actors. These threat actors seek to exacerbate societal friction to sow discord and undermine public trust in government institutions to encourage unrest, which could potentially inspire acts of violence.[19]

Notice a few funny words, "MDM," a.k.a. misinformation, disinformation, and malinformation. In other words, if you do not follow the official narrative of the rulers, you are a potential target. This is from an earlier bulletin on August 13, 2021, which stated:

> These extremists may seek to exploit the emergence of COVID-19 variants by viewing the potential re-establishment of public health restrictions across the United States as a rationale to conduct attacks. Pandemic-related stressors have contributed to increased societal strains and tensions, driving several plots by

domestic violent extremists, and they may contribute to more violence this year.[20]

Yes, you read that right. If you are like half the American population
and oppose COVID restrictions, you could be a terrorist. The same
thing applies to those questioning electoral fraud, or any issues with
mail-in ballots. You could be a terrorist!

And you know what that means in a digital world? Your financial
credits can be frozen. Your rights can be suspended. And you can wind
up in a digital gulag.

Funny how this all constantly goes full circle, right? Do you
remember when this was all just a conspiracy theory, and I was labeled
a lunatic?

Let's recap the simple model: usher everyone into having a World
ID, a vaccine passport, and digital identification. Move everyone onto
a digital financial system, tied together by a Central Bank Digital
Currency.

The digital currency will not be money.

It will be credits.

These credits will all be traceable, trackable, and tied to a Blockchain.

These financial credits can be instantly frozen, programmed to
expire, or not to work for certain products or businesses. And this whole
digital system will tie into a social credit score system that becomes
your own digital prison, unless you're deemed a "model citizen" in the
eyes of the State. But remember, this is all done for your safety, security,
and convenience.

Klaus Schwab's World Economic Forum released a report in
February 2022 titled "Advancing Digital Agency," which said: "The
COVID 19 pandemic has led to a heightened focus on the power of
medical data, specifically so-called vaccine passports. These passports
by nature serve as a form of digital identity."[21]

As you can see, this has nothing to do with health and safety. It
has nothing to do with vaccines in general. The vaccine passport is the

operating system for the World ID surveillance system. In other words, the vaccine passport is the Trojan horse for the digital gulag.

A lot of times I am accused of being sensationalizing, fearmongering, or being a plain ol' conspiracy theorist. What will happen to those EU citizens (or if this comes to the United States, as I fear it might) who don't want to participate in such an antihuman system? You won't be able to travel, or maybe like in China you can't get an airplane ticket, and/or perhaps you won't even be allowed to have money for food unless you comply with their wishes. Has there ever been a time in human history where the rulers have not tried to get away with taking the maximum amount of power possible for themselves?

The digital identity will be sold as a service that will not be mandatory. Just think how they'll try to sell it to you. The pitch will be very subtle. You don't have to submit, but if you don't, you might as well go live in the forest in a hut.

Imagine if your neighbor told you they needed an extra room in your house, but they wouldn't force you. It will just be obligatory.

The COVID-19 pandemic has provided the perfect Trojan horse for the "New Normal" digital surveillance system that will destroy your basic freedoms.

One of the most alarming things about it is the fact that nearly all global governments are pushing the same digital gulag agenda. It's almost as if the World Economic Forum has bought off and penetrated the cabinets of global governments.

Is this just a conspiracy theory?

No. Klaus Schwab said it himself during a 2018 speech!

Schwab described how his subversive World Economic Forum has, in his own words, "infiltrated" governments across the world. He states, "I have to say, when I mention now names, like Mrs. (Angela) Merkel and even Vladimir Putin, and so on, they all have been Young Global Leaders of the World Economic Forum."[22]

Therefore, it should come as no surprise that the digital gulag agenda is being rolled out in similar verbiage across the world, at the same time. And that time would be now.

\* \* \*

The Digital Identity Working Group (DIWG) chaired by Australia's Digital Transformation Agency—whose member countries also include Canada, Finland, Israel, New Zealand, Singapore, the Netherlands, the United Kingdom, and the World Bank (through observer status)— initially met in 2020 to "share experiences and opportunities for the use of digital identity initiatives."[23]

They state their agenda: "to understand how digital identity is being used and the models that might enable mutual recognition and/ or interoperability, to share respective governments' experiences with digital identity including in the COVID-19 response, and to understand what is required to enable mutual recognition and/or interoperability between DIWG member countries."[24]

The overall conclusion is that digital ID is a necessity for humans to share data in the "New Normal." The report concludes:

> Ultimately, when applied this enables the benefits unlocked by both mutual recognition and interoperability to be realized. Including more efficient government interactions, increased support for people traveling internationally. In the future, this could also feasibly enable broader recovery from COVID-19, such as strong, mutually recognized and trusted vaccination certificates to enable safer cross-border movement.[25]

Do you see how it's always about the vaccines? Vaccine passports are the Trojan horse for advancing digital identity by NGOs such as the Bill & Melinda Gates Foundation, Rockefeller Foundation, the United Nations-backed ID2020,[26] the World Bank's ID4D initiative,[27] and the World Economic Forum's "Reimagining Digital Identity: A Strategic Imperative" program.[28]

The WEF's digital gulag plan, combined with the Chinese Social Credit Score System, is the centralized foundation for a global social credit system that will give global elites total control over citizens.

* * *

Two interesting names at the forefront of this movement are Isabella Chase and Rick McDonnell. McDonnell is the executive director of ACAMS, an organization for Anti-Financial Crime professionals. His résumé also includes time at the United Nations as chief of the UN Global Program on Money Laundering.

If we just connect the dots to the Canadian Emergency Acts on Terrorism over their trucker protests, and the United States, shifting focus to combat "domestic terrorism" at home, can you see how this all ties together?

Isabella Chase is a research fellow at the Centre for Financial Crime and Security—Royal United Service Institute (RUSI). RUSI is a British think tank that works closely with the British government and military.

Isabella Chase and Rick McDonnell penned an article together in May 2021 in *American Banker* titled "The U.S. Pandemic Recovery is a Chance to Improve Digital ID." In the article, they stated:

> Digital IDs could also have supported our current recovery. For example, a digital ID system could standardize and simplify the process of scheduling a vaccination appointment, which currently varies according to state and provider. In addition, digital ID could streamline and secure individual COVID-19 vaccination records for easy verification, as well as provide backup records in the event of loss or destruction of the physical cards being issued by the CDC. Finally, "vaccine passports" or some version thereof could be achieved through the use of digital ID, at the same time ensuring the accuracy and centralization of records and preventing easily falsified physical ones.
>
> The experience of COVID-19 is a case study in the potential of digital ID as an innovative way to cut down on financial crime and identify theft, and certainly to streamline administrative processes. While issues of privacy and proper use should certainly

be debated and respected, the promise of digital ID in providing more efficiency and security makes it well worth the exploration. The sooner the U.S. embraces digital IDs, the better prepared we will be to weather the next national crisis—whatever it is and whenever it strikes.[29]

And when you remember that the vaccine passport digital ID system will be able to house your central bank digital currency wallet, then it all keeps making sense.

They used a crisis to further a long-standing agenda.

This is what I have referred to as "Problem. Reaction. Solution." A problem happens, e.g., Pandemic. The government locks everyone inside and takes away their normal way of life.

The people are afraid.

They want reassurance.

The global elites then offer a Solution, which becomes more invasive than the original problem. The "solution" is a global ID system ushered in by vaccine passports, which will be the operating system for your digital gulag. This digital gulag will host your medical, financial, and social credit score.

Of course, it's all for your own safety and convenience, right?

This is their tried-and-true formula:

Problem.

Reaction.

Solution.

And it's now being rolled out in real time with COVID-19 and the recovery.

But the goal isn't your safety.

It's about total control over our data, which will ensure our total subservience to the globalists.

## Chapter Seven

# Great Reset of Energy

We all want to save the world.
But everything has its trade-offs.

Would you willingly give up your freedom of movement, your ability to drive and to travel, if they told you it was for saving the planet? If they told you (again) that a new crisis was so severe that you had to stay inside indefinitely?

Would you be willing to allow global governments and big corporations to track and trace your every movement, in the name of saving the planet?

Would you let them automatically track your carbon based on your diet, your driving habits, and more?

If they used a military-style crackdown in the name of an emergency, would you submit to a digital surveillance system to monitor your carbon emissions?

These are questions worth asking, because this is what they want for you.

I will get to the grand plan for the climate crisis in this chapter, but let's start with the current energy crisis.

In California they've used mandates to move all their energy into renewable energy, which sounds great.

But what they've done in addition is shut down existing energy sources, without a reliable backup. In California there's three nuclear reactors. They've already shut two down. And the third, Diablo Canyon, is scheduled to be shut down in August 2025.[1] (However, the energy situation is so bad in California that Governor Newsom is currently investigating keeping Diablo Canyon beyond the scheduled closure date.)[2]

They shut down their coal power plants.

They shut down their natural gas power plants.

But guess what.

The renewables aren't close to ready yet.

So guess what happened. Shortages! The result was energy blackouts. That's why California doesn't have reliable energy, at a time when lockdowns were shutting down energy consumption. This is from the *Sacramento Bee* in May 2022, the main paper in California's state capital:

> Two years after the last wave of rolling blackouts, California officials said Friday the state could face potential shortfalls in electricity this summer as drought, extreme heat and wildfires pose threats to the fragile power grid.
>
> Leaders of the Public Utilities Commission, the state's Independent System Operator and the California Energy Commission said that state could face a shortage of as much as 1,700 megawatts—the equivalent of one major power plant—on the hottest days.[3]

In the summer of 2020, the COVID lockdowns had malls, movie theaters, and most businesses closed. Energy consumption was down, yet California still couldn't keep the lights on.

Why?

Even the liberal *Los Angeles Times* was twisting itself into pretzels of loony logic trying to explain the problems of 2020:

Careful planning to ensure adequate power supplies will become even more important as California phases out fossil fuels and moves toward 60% renewable energy by 2030 and 100% climate-friendly energy by 2045, as required by state law.

Officials have consistently said that intermittent power sources such as solar panels and wind turbines didn't cause the rolling blackouts. But gas burning power plants that can fire up when the sun isn't shining or the wind isn't blowing have been shutting down in recent years, and California has largely failed to replace them with cleaner alternatives such as lithium-ion batteries.[4]

Let's try to follow their logic. Solar panels and wind turbines didn't cause the rolling blackouts of the summer of 2020 in California. However, if there had been more gas-burning power plants, there wouldn't have been any blackouts. I guess each one of these statements is true. But they're not linked together in any rational fashion.

Why didn't the *Los Angeles Times* say something like this: "The shutting down of gas burning power plants was done before we had enough capacity with solar panels or wind turbines to cover the state's energy needs"? That sounds like it would qualify as objective journalism. We know the reason it wasn't reported like that. It would make the Democratic public officials of California look dumb. They couldn't do that. Only Republican public officials can be made fun of in the media.

And we are starting to see the exact same thing happening in the rest of the world. Now, if you haven't seen the headlines of energy outages from Asia to South America to all across Europe, then I don't know what you've been paying attention to. This mad rush to reset energy policies by engaging in some of the same reckless actions followed by the politicians in California is a cancer infecting the rest of the world.

When the former prime minister of Britain, Boris Johnson, came to the United States in September 2021 to address the United Nations, this is how the *Washington Post* described his speech:

He compared humanity to a trouble-making teen: "We have come to that fateful age when we roughly know how to drive and we know how to unlock the drinks cabinet and to engage in all sorts of activity that is not only potentially embarrassing but also terminal."

He scolded everyone for their treatment of the Earth: "This precious blue sphere with its eggshell crust and wisp of atmosphere—is not some indestructible toy, some bouncy plastic romper room against which we can hurl ourselves to our heart's content."

And he declared: "It is time for humanity to grow up."[5]

Very poetic, I'll admit. But pretty words don't make for a good plan. That seems to be the problem with the Democrats of California. Lots of poetry, but no rational plans. The *Washington Post* continued with coverage of Johnson's speech before the United Nations:

> If radical action isn't taken, he said in his address—broadcast in Britain in the early hours on Thursday morning—"we will see desertification, drought, crop failure and mass movement of humanity on a scale not seen before, not because of some unforeseen natural event or disaster but because of us, because of what we are doing now."
>
> "And our grandchildren will know we are the culprits," he said.
>
> He singled out the United States and Denmark for their pledged contributions to a $100 billion-a-year climate fund aimed at helping poorer countries cut carbon emissions and mitigate the effects of climate change. He also praised China for its pledge to end international financing of coal-fired energy plants, and he applauded Pakistan for promising to plant 10 billion trees.[6]

Let's go through Johnson's pitch. You have the warnings of terrible danger to put people into a state of fear. He demands "radical action."

Not thoughtful action. Not something well-conceived and well-executed. And is it me, or does it seem like most of these world leaders are doing everything they can to make sure they say something nice about the communist government of China, which does not allow free speech or freedom of religion? And whenever I see a hundred billion dollars a year is going to poorer countries, I always ask myself, "How much of that money is ending up in the pockets of the leaders of those countries?" Is that something unreasonable to ask?

I don't think so.

This is the plan for the Great Reset of Energy.

Let me be clear: I'm not breaking down the science of climate change. I'm not talking about carbon emissions. I'm not talking about whether it's good or bad. I'm not talking about any of that. All we're doing here is pointing out the policies that are driving this, what will come of it, and how it ties into the Great Reset.

Johnson said the United Kingdom is going to be leading by example. Ironically, they're the ones having the hardest time with it. They're the ones in an energy crisis with no safe launch pad into renewable energy. Just like California, the only place Boris Johnson is leading the United Kingdom is into a massive energy crisis. And it's already bad now.

For example, Reuters reports wholesale gas prices in the United Kingdom are up over 300 percent,[7] and CNN reports household energy costs in Britain will go up by more than eight hundred pounds (about $1,000 in American dollars) for an increase of 40 percent.[8] This was on top of an earlier increase for energy in April 2021 of 54 percent. As CNN reported:

> "This news will be utterly devastating for the 6.1 million homes currently in fuel poverty —and for the additional 1.7 million households who will spend this winter struggling to keep themselves warm," Simon Francis, coordinator for the End Fuel Poverty Coalition, a campaign group, told CNN Business.
>
> "Unless the government acts now, it will have blood on its hands this winter," he added.[9]

The poor, whom the globalists claim to care about, are the ones most hurt by these policies. Because when you can't afford your energy, it wipes out the middle class and can cause massive deaths globally.

Furthermore, in the United Kingdom there's a massive lack of fertilizer. As a result of the gas shortages, they cannot produce the fertilizer. This is how the problem was framed in November 2021 by the BBC, even before the Russian invasion of Ukraine further complicated the matter:

> Svein Tore Holsether, chief executive of Yara International, said higher gas prices were pushing up fertilizer costs and affecting food prices worldwide.
>
> Fertilizer requires large amounts of gas in its production.
>
> Mr. Holsether said Yara had been forced to cut some production due to higher gas prices, which had led to shortages.
>
> The chief executive said developing countries would be hit hardest by the shortages, with crop yields declining and food prices rising.
>
> "It's really scary, we are facing a food crisis and vulnerable people are being hit very hard," he told the BBC's Today program.[10]

As you can see, I am not exaggerating when I say that these policies are dangerous, and antihuman. The alarming thing is that these things can be happening, while Boris Johnson says they are leading by example for the rest of the world.

This is not even about debating renewables. This is just about reckless policy that's happening on a massive scale in our country with Joe Biden's Build Back Better plan. It should be obvious that when you shut down the supply of energy, but the demand's still there, it would cause serious problems. Because of course, we still need air conditioners, and we need heaters in the winter and we have to keep our food cold. We have to drive our cars.

If the demand stays, but we shut the supply down, what do you think happens? Oh yeah, it pushes the prices up, right? They are phasing out fossil fuels, and in some cases, even nuclear power. But they do not have the electrical grid infrastructure, or the reliability of green energy, to power the world.

What could be more reckless than to phase out energy that billions of people depend on for survival, without an alternative that can 100 percent take its place immediately? At this point, this should not surprise you. This is not idiocy. It's malfeasance.

The plan is simple: destroy the fossil fuel industry, send prices soaring, manufacture an energy crisis, blame fossil fuels, and shut down reliable global energy, without a viable immediate alternative. This is what the Great Reset is all about. If you want a global corporate government that rules over humanity, you have to destroy everything first.

This is a classic problem-reaction-solution.

First, you manufacture a problem by destroying American energy. You send gas prices soaring. Heating bills skyrocket. Food prices explode, because of course oil and gas are needed for the entire food supply chain. The cost of living gets out of control for the masses. It wipes out the middle class.

Then they offer the solution.

Green Energy.

The only problem, as we discussed regarding California, is that it is not capable at this time to power the world. The result is an even worse energy crisis. Because now you've stifled domestic energy production. Prices are skyrocketing. You're releasing Emergency Oil from Federal Reserves. It's not helping. People can't afford electricity or gas. The middle class is being wiped out. And instead of increasing domestic supply, you wag your finger at fossil fuels and clamor about "transitioning" to clean energy. But it's not ready.

It's as if you devise a plan to jump off your roof and land safely onto thousands of pillows.

Except the pillows haven't arrived from the store yet.

You've been cheering about "transitioning" from the roof to the ground for so long that you jump anyway. The "transition" turns into a transfer to the emergency room, and the doctor wonders why you're stupid enough to jump off a roof, if you knew the pillows weren't there. This is exactly what we're doing. The idiocy is so glaring that the only way it makes sense is if you understand the larger plan for the Great Reset.

Why else would you be dangerously jumping off roofs without a fail plan?

It should come as no surprise that you're not allowed to ask that question. In fact, it seems like Elon Musk is the only celebrity willing to discuss the obvious.

On March 4, 2022, Musk tweeted: "Hate to say it, but we need to increase oil & gas output immediately. Extraordinary times demand extraordinary measures. Obviously, this would negatively affect Tesla, but sustainable energy solutions simply cannot react instantaneously."[11]

Mark Mills is a senior fellow at the Manhattan Institute and a faculty fellow at Northwestern University's McCormick School of Engineering and Applied Science, where he codirects an Institute on Manufacturing Science and Innovation. Earlier, Mills was a technology advisor for Bank of America Securities and coauthor of the *Huber-Mills Digital Power Report*, a tech investment newsletter. In 2019, Mills published a twenty-four-page report titled "The 'New Energy Economy': An Exercise in Magical Thinking." From the report by Mills:

> So how many batteries would be needed to store, say, not two months' but two days' worth of the nation's electricity? The $5 billion Tesla "Gigafactory" in Nevada is currently the world's biggest battery manufacturing facility. Its total annual production could store three minutes' worth of annual U.S. electricity demand. Thus, in order to fabricate a quantity of batteries to store two days' worth of U.S. electricity demand would require 1,000 years of Gigafactory production . . .

Then there are the hydrocarbons and electricity needed to undertake all the mining activities and to fabricate the batteries themselves. In rough terms, it requires the energy equivalent of about 100 barrels of oil to fabricate a quantity of batteries that can store a single barrel of oil-equivalent energy.[12]

This is alarming for many reasons. First, it shows how far away we actually are from reliably powering the world on "green energy." Second, it hits on a key point that nobody discusses. It is dangerously expensive to "transition" our energy sources in the full force manner that global elites are attempting. As Mills points out in the Executive Summary of his report, it just costs more. A lot more. Six times more:

> Scientists have yet to discover, and entrepreneurs have yet to invent, anything as remarkable as hydrocarbons in terms of the combination of the low-cost, high-energy density, stability, safety, and portability. In practical terms, this means that spending $1 million on utility-scale wind turbines, or solar panels will each, over 30 years of operation, produce about 50 million kilowatt-hours (kWh)—while an equivalent $1 million spent on a shale rig produces enough natural gas over 30 years to generate over 300 million kWh.[13]

How are they going to actually implement all this?

Well, of course, they are going to print the money out of thin air.

We already saw what has happened since COVID-19 lockdowns. Global governments printed astronomical amounts of fiat currency, and we're now experiencing dangerous levels of inflation with no end in sight (more on this later). But now they want to totally eliminate our only source of reliable energy, without their "clean" energy being ready.

So what exactly will they do to complete their "transition"?

They will simply print trillions and trillions of dollars.

The money will go to all their cronies.

Backdoor deals.

Stock options.

Lining the pockets of everybody "in the know."

Trillions of new currency units will be chasing even fewer products and services, since we already have supply chain disasters. Historic inflation levels will go much higher. The politicians will virtue signal about saving the world, and you will be eating crushed-up bugs from a drone delivered directly to your house that's owned by BlackRock! Oh, and you'll be having rolling blackouts because the power grid cannot sustain us this way. Anything to save the world, right?

These rallying cries for climate emergency and energy crises are the perfect way to continue consolidating power.

\* \* \*

While it may seem like a sci-fi fantasy, soon the United States federal government could force automakers to install kill switches authorities can access and use to shut down any newer vehicle.

On January 5, 2022, Steve Symes of Yahoo News wrote an article titled "New Law Will Install Kill Switches In All New Cars." Yes, that is real, and it's directly from the Biden Administration's Infrastructure bill. Here's what Symes wrote:

> According to an article written by former U.S. Representative Bob Barr, hidden away in the recently passed infrastructure bill, the very one I warned before would negatively impact drivers across the country if it were to pass, is a measure to install vehicle kill switches into every new car, truck, and SUV sold in this country. The regulation likely won't be enforced for five years, so maybe there's time to do something about this . . .
>
> . . . But wait, there's more. The kill switch "safety" system would be open, or in other words there would be a backdoor. That would allow police or other government authorities to access it whenever. Would they need a warrant to do that? Likely not.

Even better, hackers could access the backdoor and shut down your vehicle.[14]

It would seem that not only do the globalists want to mess up the world's energy supply, but if you happen to be in your vehicle, they'd also like to exercise control over you.

And there's more.

That very same infrastructure bill includes a pilot program to track your vehicle miles.

Tucked away on page 508 of the US Senate's 2,700-page, so-called "infrastructure" bill are the plans for a national "per mile fee" pilot program. And it is exactly what it sounds like—the more you drive, the more you pay. Of course, this will ultimately make travel too costly for those who are not global elites. But even more concerning than the fees are the security and privacy concerns. Possible recording methods listed in the bill include:

- Third-party on-board diagnostic (OBD-II) devices
- Smartphone applications
- Telemetric data collected by automakers
- Motor vehicle data obtained by car insurance companies
- Data from the States that received a grant under section 6020 of the FAST Act
- Motor vehicle data obtained from fueling stations
- Any other method that the Secretary considers appropriate[15]

Ultimately, I believe that the microchips and digital software in your car will sync to your personal identity, just like your iPhone syncs to your iCloud. Your car will become a surveillance device to monitor, track, trace, and penalize you. And in a digital world, it will be automatically synced with your digital currency financial accounts and social credit score.

Perhaps this is another reason why they want us all to use electric cars?

* * *

By the way, how are you feeling digesting all this information?

I know it's a lot to absorb and can feel a bit overwhelming.

So let's have a little laugh while on the subject of the climate change emergency. Now, if you still don't believe that the global elite are deranged lunatics who will trample your basic human rights in the name of saving the planet, get a load of this headline from the *Huffington Post*: "Could a Small Nuclear War Reverse Global Warming?"

> Nuclear war is a bad thing.
>
> Right?
>
> Scientists from NASA and a number of other institutions have recently been modeling the effects of a war involving a hundred Hiroshima-level bombs, or 0.03 percent of the world's current nuclear arsenal, according to National Geographic.
>
> The result, according to NASA climate models, could actually be global cooling.[16]

Ah yes, just nuke the world, kill millions of people, and we will have far fewer carbon footprints. What a genius idea by such an acclaimed media outlet! Why didn't we think of this idea earlier? Why isn't every politician just campaigning for global nuclear war as the best way to save the planet and reverse climate change?

In the 1980s, during the height of the campaign against nuclear weapons, there was a popular bumper sticker that read, "A nuclear bomb could ruin your whole day."

Apparently, that may not be the case for the globalists.

Whether it's a "climate crisis" or a "financial crisis," these are opportunities for a consolidation of power. As I've explained, the overall goal is simple: collapse the first world through massive inflation, energy crises, and food shortages.

As the first world collapses, so does the third world. Then, they will send hundreds of millions of "climate refugees" into the collapsing first world. This will totally collapse global civilization. It will be blamed on an unfair economic system (one they prospered from) and climate change.

This is when they can fully institute the Great Reset and begin to completely Build Back Better. For over two decades, I've been speaking to this exact plan. They will destroy reliable energy, blame it on a variety of events, from Putin to inflation to greedy energy producers. The cost of living will get out of control. They will use this as a cover for an "energy transition," in which they will print tens of trillions of dollars to build a "greener economy."

Inflation will get even worse. And we do not have the mining and exploration capabilities to cheaply convert the world to their green energy system, so commodity prices will continue to skyrocket. Food shortages. Out-of-control energy prices. A collapse of the third world. This will be the cover for "climate refugees," because of course, they will never take any blame.

They will simply point the finger at climate change, displacing hundreds of millions of people, moving them into further extreme poverty, and shutting off the global resources.

Biden's climate czar, John Kerry (who flies around on private jets while lecturing us on using less energy), has painted the picture before. He said, "Wait until you see 100 million people for whom the entire food production capacity has collapsed."[17]

And with energy prices rising at uncontrollable levels, and food prices skyrocketing, this is only the beginning. But the global elites do not seem interested in getting energy prices under control. In fact, it seems to be the opposite.

But don't take my word for it.

For example, the president of the European Union Commission, Ursula von der Leyen, summed it up quite nicely in her speech at the World Economic Forum's Davos event. On January 20, 2022, she tweeted a clip of a recent speech for the billionaire crowd at Davos. In incredible irony, the background of her speech carried corporate logos for "Davos Agenda" and "World Economic Forum." She tweeted out part of her speech and said,

Today's gas crisis must serve to accelerate the transition to clean energy. For this, we also need trust. People need to trust that the transition will be fair. Businesses, that it will improve their competitiveness. And investors, that we will stay the course. #DavosAgenda.[18]

But don't worry, she says we need to "trust that the transition will be fair."

Surely, if you're ever going to trust someone to reset the global energy systems of the world, it's going to be the billionaire crowd, right?

The Great Reset on energy is just another way for the Davos crowd to steal your power.

\* \* \*

In an address in November 2021 to world leaders at the COP26 Climate Summit in Glasgow, Scotland, Prince Charles set the tone for other world leaders regarding the climate.

As you read it, see if you can play a little game and catch all the globalist buzz words. Here is what CNBC reported about his comments:

> Prince Charles, addressing delegates at the summit, says the Covid-19 pandemic has demonstrated just how devastating a global cross-border threat can be.
>
> "Climate change and biodiversity loss are no different—in fact they pose an even greater existential threat, to the extent we have to put ourselves on what might be called a war-like footing," he says.
>
> He calls for a radical transformation of our fossil fuel-based economy to one that is genuinely renewable and sustainable.[19]

He sures sounds a lot like the rest of the gang! There's a lot of buzz words in there: *Existential threat. War-like footing. Radical transformation.*

They need you to believe there is an existential threat, and we need to do something.

It's a crisis.

They must seize this crisis and make it go to good use. They will do this with "war-like footing." But remember, folks, when the health organizations declare it an emergency of public health and attempt to use the fear of death to take away your freedoms again, it's for saving the world.

If you haven't noticed yet, the global elite's plan is always to declare something an emergency, an existential threat, something that could kill you! This fear they inject into the population is how they attempt to morally justify using "war-like footing" to take away your freedoms and continue on the path of the Great Reset.

And what did President Joe Biden say at this meeting? Here's what CNBC reported:

> U.S. President Joe Biden warned in his COP26 speech on Monday that "in an age where this pandemic has made so painfully clear that no nation can wall itself off from borderless threats, we know that none of us can escape the worst that's yet to come if we fail to seize this moment."
>
> Biden added that "within the growing catastrophe I believe there's an incredible opportunity, not just for the United States but for all of us."[20]

So what do you think they have planned? It's not something we're going to enjoy. I can tell you that much!

This is why it's so important we continue to learn their plans and wake up the masses!

Thankfully, there's been a lot of great coverage on climate change lockdowns and the power grab that will ensue from elites declaring a climate crisis as a health emergency.

One of the people providing that coverage is Tucker Carlson. Tucker has admirably covered the prospects of climate lockdowns.

Here is the transcript of a great dialogue Carlson had on his show from June 22, 2021:

> **Tucker Carlson:** So we're learning more now about the sad toll of the corona lockdowns in this country. According to Biden, though, we could get another round of lockdowns. These for a crisis that's every bit as bad as the coronavirus, maybe worse. That crisis, of course, says Joe Biden, is climate change.

> **President Joe Biden (video clip speech transcript of Biden):** Today, I'm pleased to announce the team that will lead my administration's ambitious plan to address the existential threat of our time, climate change. Folks, we're in a crisis. Just like we need to be a unified nation in response to COVID-19, we need a unified national response to climate change, and from this crisis, from these crises I should say, we need to seize an opportunity to build back and build back better than we were before.[21]

I will criticize most of the mainstream media, but Tucker Carlson stands head and shoulders above most of the commentators. Notice how people like President Biden try to ingratiate themselves to you by being nonthreatening. "Folks, we're in a crisis." He sounds just like your favorite uncle:

> **Tucker Carlson:** A unified national response? It's involuntary, that's the one thing we know. What does it mean? Well, we're learning that a World Health Organization staffer has written a report saying that a climate lockdown could be called for, just like a COVID lockdown, a climate lockdown.
>
> Marc Morano is an author who has written a lot about climate change. He founded Climate Depot. He joins us tonight. Marc, thanks so much for coming on. A climate lockdown, now, I would laugh this off the table, except we all just lived through

the last 18 months, so we know that anything is possible. What does this mean exactly?

**Marc Morano:** Well, in my book, *Green Fraud*, I detail two chapters on this, Tucker. The climate activists were, first of all, jealous when the COVID lockdowns happened. They were beside themselves saying, "How is this happening?"

Everyone from Greta Thunberg, to John Kerry, UN officials, and then they started saying, "We need to follow this. If we can shut down for a virus, we can shut down for climate," and that's what we're seeing. There are even academics in Australia proposing adding climate change to death certificates, and Bill Gates has said the death toll will be greater.

So, they're following every step of the way, and it's not just a professor here, or someone in academia. We have a major UK report coming out, we have an international agency report that came out calling for essentially the same type of lockdowns. Everything from restrictions on your thermostat, to restrictions of moving. You can only fly in a climate emergency when it's quote, "morally justifiable."

Kind of like a lockdown, you have to justify going to the store for essential services. They're going after freedom of movement, they're going after private car ownership, they're going after everything it means to be a free person and turning it over to the administrative state.[22]

There's a great deal in that exchange of which people need to take notice. These globalists always seem to get on the same page. Seriously, have you ever seen these globalists get into a fight with each other, as conservatives often do? Tucker continued:

**Tucker Carlson:** Would this include shutting down the iPhone factories in China? Would China and India participate in this climate lockdown, or is it kind of "You first, America?"

**Marc Morano:** Well, as we know, the [COVID] lockdowns had never been proposed. We felt like lemmings following the Chinese Communist Party in terms of them recommending lockdowns. The World Health Organization went after it, the World Health Organization employees are now recommending these climate lockdowns. The one country that won't be affected is China, as you say. As we're sitting home binge watching Netflix, we're not going to be able to have the freedoms we used to have.

In the UK, they proposed $CO_2$ ration cards that the government or employers would monitor your $CO_2$ levels, your energy use, your travel, the type of car you drive. If you exceed a level, you pay penalties. If you're under, you get credits. This is the world. A $CO_2$ budget for every man, woman, and child on the planet has been proposed by a German climate advisor. This is what we're looking at.

I talked to a German who talked about East Germany. They used to have these kinds of restrictions in East Germany before you could leave the country, but we're talking about proposing these now on Americans within the country, and we had this, of course, with COVID. They were talking about bans on interstate travel at one point, a national ban, some of Biden's advisors. So, anything is possible. Chuck Schumer is urging Biden to declare a national climate emergency. Just like a blue state governor, he could have emergency powers.[23]

It would be difficult to find a more succinct conversation on the subject. Tucker plays the dreary clip of Joe Biden speaking a lot like the rest of the global elites. He uses words (just like Prince Charles): "the existential threat of our time, climate change. Folks, we're in a crisis. Just like we need to be a unified nation in response to COVID-19, we need a unified national response to climate change, [and from these crises] we need to seize an opportunity to build back. And build back better than we were before."

But there's something even more interesting.

If you compare Prince Charles's quotes with Joe Biden's, they are eerily similar.

Now here goes the conspiracy theorist in me.

Does it seem far-fetched to suggest the same group wrote those speeches for the two men?

By now, it should be clear that when Biden says it's a crisis, and we need to seize the opportunity, he's referring to Obama's former Chief-of-Staff Rahm Emmanuel's philosophy: "You never want a serious crisis to go to waste. And what I mean by that is an opportunity to do things that you think you could not do before."[24]

In my opinion, Biden's Build Back Better is simply the global elite's sanctioned political slogan for the Great Reset.

But it's not just me, Tucker Carlson, Prince Charles, and Joe Biden saying that it's coming. On September 12, 2021, the *New York Post* published an article titled "Get Ready for Climate Change Lockdowns":

> A recent *Nature* journal piece notes, COVID-19 lockdowns have prepared people for "personal carbon allowances." Restrictions on your individual freedoms "that were unthinkable only one year before" have us "more prepared to accept the tracking and limitations" to "achieve a safer climate."[25]

And there's those pesky little words again; "personal carbon allowances" and "tracking and limitations."

But it doesn't stop there: *The Guardian* wrote a piece with the following title and subtitle: "Equivalent of Covid emissions drop needed every two years—study: Equivalent falls in emissions over a decade required to keep to safe limits of global heating, experts say." Here's the opening of that piece:

> Carbon dioxide emissions must fall by the equivalent of a global lockdown roughly every two years for the next decade for the world to keep within safe limits of global heating, research has shown.

Lockdowns around the world led to an unprecedented fall in emissions of about 7% in 2020, or about 2.6 billion tons of $CO_2$, but reductions of between 1 billion and 2 billion tons are needed every year of the next decade to have a good chance of holding temperature rises to within 1.5C or 2C of pre-industrial levels, as required by the Paris agreement.[26]

How about some programming with your news? Don't you like how they say, "carbon dioxide emissions must fall?" The globalists want you to agree with them.

A similar theme was echoed in a *Forbes* article from March 2021 titled "Report: World Needs Equivalent of Pandemic Lockdown Every Two Years to Meet Paris Carbon Emission Goals."[27]

Now is this starting to seem like it actually is a secret agenda by a group (global elites) to do something harmful? And it's worth noting these are the exact messaging points of Klaus Schwab and the World Economic Forum! This is taken from one of their publications from January 2022, titled "The Great Acceleration: What We Need to Do to Tackle Climate Change":

> Governments, too, can promote the acceleration of climate action. They can join the nations championing a global price on $CO_2$, which would spark investment in climate-friendly technologies. And carbon pricing, implemented globally would eliminate concerns that climate action costs too much or has a negative impact on competitiveness. It would level the playing field and allow the private sector to focus on the real issue: accelerating the transition to sustainable value chains.
>
> Another action governments can take to tackle climate change is to invest in large-scale green infrastructure and to encourage private investors to do the same. Green infrastructure is an investment in the future and wise use of pandemic recovery funds.[28]

One thing should be clear: they are carefully planting the psychological seeds to prepare you for massive government overreach and an invasion of your human rights, in the name of saving the planet. We know where this leads: carbon tracking and tracing of your movements, just like COVID-19.

But of course, this will all be for your health and safety!

\* \* \*

How does the big plan all get put together?

Why, by tying together your vaccine passport with your carbon footprint. What an excellent way to manage the population. This is from *Vox* in March 2021, helpfully explaining the dual use of this technology:

> While the Commons Project is attracting a growing number of partners, it isn't the only vaccine passport maker out there. Beyond its work on New York's Excelsior Pass, which was tested at Madison Square Garden and the Barclays Center, IBM is working with Germany to produce digital versions of its paper vaccine certificates. The International Air Transport Association (IATA) is also developing its own "Travel pass" for airlines, which is now being tested by Virgin Atlantic, Emirates, and other carriers. Carbon Health plans to expand the functionality of its Health Pass to work with Apple Wallet and Google Pay. Even Mastercard has joined the fray; it's working with the International Chamber of Commerce on a protocol for a "global, interoperable health pass system."[29]

Once they get your approval to be tracked for COVID-19, it's not that big of a jump to get you to agree to track your carbon footprint.

However, one shouldn't think these plans are inevitable, as when Michael Evans, president of Alibaba Group USA, spoke about just such a device on May 24, 2022, at the World Economic Forum in Davos, Switzerland:

> It's another high-tech method for tracking human behavior, and China is already widely known to be violating the human rights of its citizens with a social credit system of tracking, so the fact that the technology is coming from the Alibaba Group is raising alarms.
>
> In the video posted to twitter, Evans told the audience, "We're developing, through technology, an ability for consumers to measure their whole carbon footprint."
>
> "What does that mean?" he asked. "Where they are traveling. How they are traveling. What are they eating. What they are consuming on the platform. So individual carbon footprint tracker," as a surprised reaction can be heard in the video coming from the audience.[30]

It can be overwhelming to fully understand the plan of the globalists, but they count on you not being informed, or being so enamored of their promises that you won't question some of the more troubling aspects.

But the truth is their plans are fragile.

All we need to do is speak out, stand up, say no to them, and they will have to flee from us and civilized society.

## Chapter Eight

# Great Reset of Food

The mainstream media is now warning us that it's time to get ready for food shortages and food rationing.

Of course, they're blaming Putin for the food crisis.

But you and I know better.

We're entering a frontier with threats from many dimensions; inflation, supply chains collapsing, food shortages, fertilizer shortages, and a global energy crisis.

This is a global food crisis. It will hit every country in the world. People like me have been warning that it was coming and was being intentionally created, dating back to the original COVID lockdowns in March 2020.

But this is the frame I want you to put on this issue. Every time one of the globalists tries to implement some part of their plan, such as an attack on our supply chain for food, there are a thousand people like you and me trying to fix the problem. They may not understand what's happening on the global level. But they know much better than the globalists how to fix things in their small corner of the world. All these tiny victories will lead to a much larger one.

Now we're seeing Joe Biden say that food shortages are real.[1] Countries are beginning to restrict exports of their food. In fact, just at the time of writing this chapter, to secure the supply of basic food goods, the government of Moldova banned the exports of grain and sugar (effective after March 1, 2022).[2] To prevent market failures, it extended the price regulations from baked goods to other basic goods: pork, frozen fish, poultry, beets, white cabbage, eggs, and pasta.

Reuters reported that Hungary followed suit shortly thereafter and banned the export of grains.[3] Hungary is a big producer of grains and a net exporter. So when they ban exports of grains, that means that there are other countries that are net importers who will not have food.

Those who have grains are no longer giving it away. And those who don't will soon find themselves in the middle of a dangerous food crisis. This is how the Reuters news agency described the problem in June 2022:

> Russia and Ukraine together account for nearly a third of global wheat supply, and their importance has been underscored by an Indian export ban as well as adverse crop weather in North America and Western Europe.
>
> The war, together with Western sanctions against Russia, have sent the price of grain, cooking oil, fertilizer and energy soaring.
>
> Ukraine is also a major exporter of corn, barley, sunflower oil and rapeseed oil, while Russia and Belarus—which has backed Moscow in the war and is also under sanctions—account for over 40% of global exports of the crop nutrient potash.[4]

It's getting so serious that recently the European Union had a meeting with their agricultural ministers and is enacting an EU food crisis contingency plan, a crisis mechanism to monitor a food shortage.[5]

But the truth is that they don't really have a plan. The only plan is to blame climate change, greedy capitalists, urge us to stop eating meat, and start tracking our carbon footprints. Of course, they will do all of this while flying on private jets to meet in private to discuss how to save us all.

On my daily radio show, I've talked extensively about the United Nations discussing global food rationing. Now at the time of writing this, it's the year 2022.

Joe Biden has said about food shortages: "It's going to be real."

However, much as I hate to tell you this, it's only the beginning. In April 2022, an article from the *Western Standard Online* documented the dozens of food facilities that have caught on fire across the United States in Spring 2022. The author of the piece, Melanie Risdon, wrote beautifully about what's been happening:

> Food shortages have been exacerbated by a string of fires, plane crashes and explosions at nearly two dozen food processing facilities across Canada and the US. The most recent happened on Thursday in Georgia when a small plane crashed shortly after takeoff into a General Mills plant just east of Atlanta. Two occupants of the plane were killed in the crash, as reported by the *New York Post*.
>
> A massive fire on Monday night destroyed parts of the Azure Standard Headquarters in Oregon, a company that self-describes as "the USA's largest independent food distributor."
>
> The company said, "basically any liquid product," such as honey, oil, and vinegar, will be out of stock due to the fire, as reported by *Vision Times*.
>
> The company also said it lost its fruit packing and carob product facility in the blaze but said the effects will be minimal as fruit harvesting season hasn't started yet.[6]

Two dozen food processing plants across the country have had problems, including one where a plane crashed into the plant. Sounds a little mysterious, don't you think? But again, see how even though this incident happened, those on the ground are figuring a way around the problem. Risdon continued:

Last Thursday, firefighters contended with a massive blaze at Taylor Farms packaged salad plant in Salinas, Calif.—a key agricultural region 177 km south of San Francisco. The fire broke out late Wednesday night, as reported by *KTLA*.

That same day, an airplane crashed into Idaho's Gem State Processing facility—a plant said to process 18,000 acres worth of potatoes each year. The pilot of the plane did not survive, however, no employees were injured, reported *Vision Times*.

On April 13, firefighters from several departments in Maine helped battle a massive fire that destroyed East Conway Beef & Pork butcher shop and meat market in Center Conway, N.H.

Investigators did not indicate what caused the fire, reported *ABC* affiliate *WMTW* in Portland, Maine.[7]

Add into the mix a suspicious fire and a second airplane crashing into a food processing plant, and you might have something that would draw the attention of Sherlock Holmes:

In March, KAIT TV reported a major fire that forced the closure of the Nestle plant in Jonesboro, Ark. The plant makes frozen foods, particularly Hot Pockets. The frozen foods plant announced its plans for a $100 million expansion last year.

The Penobscot McCrum potato processing facility in Belfast, Maine, was also destroyed by fire in March. Officials believe a deep-fryer was behind the fire, as reported by *ABC* affiliate *WMTW News 8*.

In Canada, fire crews and paramedics responded after an explosion at the Centre de valorisation de l'aliment de l'Estrie, an industrial food preparation and processing facility in Sherbrooke, Que. Five people were injured in the March explosion that turned into a major fire.[8]

Plane crashes, fires, and explosions. Nothing out of the ordinary to see here. I'm sure it's all a coincidence. No reason to scare the children.

And, in late March, a fire at the Maricopa Food Pantry, a food bank in Arizona, saw 50,000 pounds worth of food burn up and yet another blaze at the Texas-based Rio Fresh severely damaged the onion processing facility.

In February, a portion of Wisconsin River Meats was destroyed by fire, according to *Channel 3000 News*. The Mauston-based company said the "old portion" of its plant was a total loss from the fire.

Another fire in February, sparked by a boiler explosion at a potato chip plant south of Hermiston, Ore., sent several people to hospital with minor injuries. The Shearer's Food plant, as reported by *The Oregonian*, supplies much of the Western US with potato and corn chips.

A third fire in February caused the Louis Dreyfus Company's Claypool, Ind., soybean processing and biodiesel plant — the largest fully integrated soybean processing plant in the US—to suspend production. Thankfully no injuries were reported.[9]

I understand that some people might wonder how this period of time compares to other periods of time. Maybe this is just usual. Maybe this is some kind of cyberwarfare being waged by China or Russia. Who would know? If this was sabotage, the entire point would be to do it in a way that did not rouse the American public, right?

A blaze at a poultry processing plant in the Hamilton region of Ontario in January caused extensive damage but caused no injuries. The multiple-alarm fire, as reported by *Global News*, will cost millions in repairs.

Firefighters responded to a fire in January at the Cargill-Nutrena plant in Lecompte, La. The fire took more than 12 hours to put out, as reported by *KALB-TV*, an *NBC/CBS/CW*-affiliated television station.

A fire in December caused more than $100,000 in damages to a San Antonio food processing plant. *KTSA-107.1* reported there were no injuries as a result of the fire.

In late November, a fire engulfed the Maid-Rite Steak Co. food processing plant in Lackawanna County, Pennsylvania, as reported by *ABC* affiliate news station *WNEP* . The cause of the fire was ruled an accident.[10]

I understand that when you read the litany of incidents at food-processing plants it's easy to be disheartened. These people seem so powerful. But I'm sure at every one of those plants, the salt-of-the-earth, good American working people are fixing things. They are our greatest weapon and that should never be forgotten. The article finished up the litany of suspicious incidents:

A fire in mid-September at the JBS USA beef processing plant in Grand Island, Neb. halted operations in the facility that typically processes about 6,000 head of cattle daily.

Although the fire damaged a portion of the facility, the company, at the time, released a statement that said the fire did not impact the primary production area, as reported by *Reuters*.

Another raging fire in August of 2021 severely damaged the Patak Meat Production company in Austell, Ga., as reported by *Channel 2 Action News* in Atlanta.

According to the company's customer service department, Patak Meat Production is operating at a "much reduced" capacity, but hopes to complete repairs in the coming months and will then regain full operational capacity.

In July, Firefighters battled a large fire at the River Valley Ingredients plant in Hanceville, Al. The cause of the fire, as reported at the time by *NBC* affiliate *WVTM-TV*, was unknown.

Another July fire at the Kellogg factory in Memphis, Tenn. was determined to be an accident and no injuries were reported.

Dozens of crews were called in to help fight the fire due to the brutal heat, reported *Fox 13 Memphis*.

The cause of a fire in April 2021 at the Smithfield Foods plant in Monmouth, Ill, was unknown, according to *WGIL-93.7FM* in Galesburg.[11]

As I've stated for many years on my radio show, the global elite's plan is to destabilize the global food supply in order to fully control the population and institute the Great Reset. You can take the succinct summary from Melanie Risdon, who documents dozens of food plants that have mysteriously been destroyed as simply a coincidence.

But what we cannot debate is that it's quite peculiar.

For the longest time food prices remained stable in the United States and consumers were not particularly concerned about price fluctuations each month. As far back as we can remember, our supermarkets were packed with food, and something that always made grocers proud was their ability to ensure an enormous variety for their customers. But now we can see that things are a whole lot different, and not in a good way.

As the world tries to rebound from the global recession induced by the COVID lockdowns, a massive wave of inflation is dramatically hitting agricultural commodities, and food producers are having to pass those cost increases to consumers. However, many industry experts have been warning that the recent price hikes won't be the only ones. In fact, they are marking the beginning of a prolonged era of higher prices and low supply. This means that although we are already facing some painful food inflation, prices won't get any lower than they are at this moment for a long, long time. When we look forward, several events that are unfolding right now will likely combine and contribute to the acceleration of food price inflation in the coming months.

In addition to the curious accidents at food-production facilities, gas prices are hitting record highs every month, and it's become way more expensive to transport food around the country. Supply transportation costs have already been going up due to a national shortage of drivers. As CNN reported on May 30, 2022, just as the summer driving season was getting started:

> The national average of regular gasoline rose to a fresh record of $4.62 a gallon on Monday, according to AAA. That's up a penny from Sunday and 44 cents more expensive than a month ago.
>
> Gas prices are up sharply from last Memorial Day, when they averaged $3.05 a gallon, according to AAA.
>
> Seven states are now averaging $5-a-gallon gas, with the latest being Illinois (rounded up from $4.996). New York and Arizona are just pennies away from hitting that milestone. And there are no states where gas prices average less than $4.10 a gallon.[12]

As a consequence, companies will have no choice but to pass these added costs onto consumers.

Not to mention the ruthless megadrought in the Western states just continues to get worse. Many areas haven't experienced such an extreme drought in more than twenty years, going back to 2000.[13] In many states water levels are dropping dangerously low, and *Smithsonian* magazine reports the Colorado River basin is experiencing a twelve-hundred-year megadrought.[14]

Furthermore, the shipping and supply-chain issues are not going away. Ryan Johnson, a twenty-year veteran in the trucking industry, revealed in a recent article published by *Medium*:

> I have a simple question for every expert who thinks they understand the root causes of the shipping crisis. Why is there only one crane for every 50 to 100 trucks at every port in America? No expert will answer this question. I'm a class A truck driver with experience in nearly every aspect of freight. My experience in the trucking industry of 20 years tells me that nothing is going to change in the shipping industry.[15]

The trucking industry veteran pointed out that one of the main reasons why most trucking companies don't want anything to do with transporting shipping containers is the fact that port operations have always been extremely messy, and things have gotten a whole lot worse since the beginning of the COVID lockdowns:

> I've waited up to eight hours in the first line just to get into the port. It's a rare day when a driver gets in and out in under two hours. By 'rare day', I mean maybe a handful of times a year," Johnson explains. "Ports don't have enough workers to keep operations fluid, no matter whether you are in a coastal or inland union or non-union port. The situation is the same all over the nation.[16]

Johnson, for his part, is a union driver paid by the hour; however, most port drivers are independent contractors leased onto a carrier who's paying them by the load. That means whether their load takes two hours, fourteen hours, or three days to complete, they get paid the same rate. On top of that, they have to pay at least 90 percent of their truck operating expenses, and companies usually cover less than 10 percent of the remaining expenses.

In short, nonunion drivers are paid extremely low rates for ship and container transport, and they have to cover all their own repairs and fuel and all truck-related expenses. Johnson reveals:

> I honestly don't understand how many of them can even afford to show up for work. In some cases, they work 70-hour weeks and they still end up owing money to their carrier. That's why when ports started to get congested due to the impacts of the health crisis last spring, the vast majority of drivers refused to show up. . . . In a few weeks, congestion got so bad that of being able to do three loads a day, they could only do one. They took a two-third pay cut. Most of the drivers were working 12 hours a day or

more while carriers were charging increased shipping rates. None of those rate increases went to driver wages. Many drivers simply quit. However, while the pickup rate for containers severely decreased, they were still being offloaded from the boats, and it's only gotten worse.

The experts want to say we can do things like open the ports 24/7, and the problem will be over in a couple of weeks. But getting a container out of the port, as slow and aggravating as it is, is really the easy part if you can find a truck and chassis to haul it, but every truck driver in America cannot operate 24/7. Even if the government suspends hours of service regulations, a federal regulation determining how many hours a week we can work or drive, we still need to sleep at some point.[17]

There's always something so refreshing when reading an account of somebody who knows the subject about which they write. This is how it looks on the ground to the regular workers. Even though they shouldn't be working. But that's not the American worker. He or she will work, even if the pay is low, because there is dignity in work:

Legally, truck drivers can work 14 hours a day, which is already excessively long. Most of them are already doing that. There's a limited amount of trucks and qualified drivers in the market, and the solution the government's now proposing is to make them work 24 hours a day every day and not stop until the backlog is cleared. It's simply not realistic. And it's physically impossible. If you can't get a container unloaded at a warehouse, having drivers work 24 7, 365 solves nothing. We need tens of thousands, more chassis and a much greater capacity in trucking. Many supply eye chain workers are paid minimum wages. They get no benefits. There's a high rate of turnover, because the physical conditions can be brutal.

Right now, it's all failing spectacularly together, but fixing one piece won't do anything. It all needs to be fixed, and at the same time. How do you convince truckers to work when their pay is not guaranteed, even to the point where they lose money?[18]

The regular person working as a truck driver has a perspective on the trucking crisis that is better than that of any secretary of transportation:

> My prediction is that nothing is going to change, and the shipping crisis is only going to get worse. Nobody in the supply chain wants to pay to solve the problem. At this point, the backlogs are so extensive that the backlogs themselves are prompting container companies, ports, warehouses, and trucking companies to charge massive rate increases for doing literally nothing to ease the situation. Given that, the ones operating ports, shipping containers, warehouses, and trucking companies are not willing to pay the workers any more than they did over the last year. The entire industry is basically setting back and chasing in on the huge mess they have created. In fact, the more things are backed up, the more every point of the supply chain cashes in. There is literally no incentive to change, even if it means consumers have to do holiday shopping in July and pay triple for shipping.[19]

Now you can see some truth in the comment from Henry Kissinger: "Who controls the food supply controls the people; who controls the energy can control whole continents; who controls money can control the world."[20]

John Kerry, the former senator and 2004 Democratic nominee for president and now Biden's climate czar, said: "Wait until you see 100 million people for whom the entire food production capacity has collapsed."[21]

But it will not be climate change that brings about this collapse.

It will be the plan of the globalists.

\* \* \*

Essentially, what's happening is that we've destroyed the supply chain during COVID lockdowns. Now, global fertilizer exports are being destroyed from the Russian/Ukraine conflict. Tucker Carlson has been covering it extensively, and I want to quote a segment of his show here:

> **Tucker Carlson:** Wait to hear what's about to happen to fertilizer, which is the basis of food. Turns out Russia doesn't simply supply energy to the entire world, it is a major supplier of every crop nutrient farmers need. That means thanks to American European sanctions your grocery bill is about to get much, much bigger. Ben Riensche is an expert on the subject, he owns and runs the Blue Diamond Farming Company in Iowa, he farms more than 16,000 acres in the state. So again, he would know. Ben Riensche joins us tonight. Ben, thanks so much for coming on. It's embarrassing how little most people know about fertilizer, where it comes from, what it means. But tell us the implications of these sanctions.

> **Ben Riensche:** Soaring fertilizer prices are likely to bring spiked food prices. If you're upset that gas is up a dollar or two a gallon, wait until your grocery bill is up $1,000 a month. It might not just manifest itself in terms of price, it could be quantity as well. Empty shelf syndrome may just be starting.[22]

There you have the perfect globalist plan. Collapse the food production system in some manner, consolidate what remains, then take control over the food supply. I know Tucker and I may see things slightly differently, but even with his cautious approach, he seemed troubled:

> **Tucker Carlson:** I'm sorry. I just want to make sure I heard you correctly, up $1,000 a month?

> **Ben Riensche:** Sure. The price of growing my crops or the major crops of corn, soybean, wheat, rice, cotton are up 30 to 40, they

are on my farm and most of that is fertilizer. Nitrogen prices are up three times from the last crop we put in, phosphorus and potassium are doubled. The planting season in the Northern Hemisphere is just weeks away, there's no miracle technology that can cut that in half or a third. It's a pretty fixed formula. For me to grow an acre of corn on my farm I need 200 pounds of nitrogen, 200 pounds of phosphorus and 100 pounds of potash. It's going to be hard how this plays out, will farmers switch to other crops that produce less? We're certainly not going to literally pour on the groceries to grow this crop.[23]

People who are involved in agriculture understand there's a certain way in which food need to be grown. It may not be as simple as simply telling people to grow more food:

**Tucker Carlson:** I mean, it's only food. Are you saying this is an essential product for people?

**Ben Riensche:** Well it pretty much is, and there's some pretty likely culprits on this. As you detailed, the number one thing is natural gas. It's the key stock of most fertilizer inputs, especially ammonium fertilizer inputs. But then we've got supply chains lows that came from the pandemic, a few hurricanes that knocked down some supply sources. But what's really affecting us is the things that could have been prevented, the ESG things. This could kind of be described as the food crisis of the Green New Deal.

To elaborate, policies that have made us more dependent on foreign energy, energy plants that have been decommissioned from other power sources and transitioned to natural gas and thus competing against the fertilizer input stocks. Wall Street taking an activist investor role with strategic plant closures.

But the kingpin in this, the worst part for a farmer, is this action that's been taken by the International Trade Commission,

tariffs that they put in place creating monopolies that we can't
buy from friendly parties [that] have a third of the supplies.[24]

Henry Kissinger warned us when he said: "Control the Food, control
the People. Control the Energy, control the Continents. Control the
Money, control the World."

We've already discussed their goal to control energy, people, and
countries. Later, we will take about their strategy in controlling the
money. Now let's talk about what Henry Kissinger said first: "Control
the food."

Now I have to warn you.

This is a bit scary.

But of course, you can handle it, because you want a better world.

What's going on? What are the real motivations behind this, who
are the players involved, and of course, most importantly, what are the
implications for this for our own health and for the future of the country and for the world?

They're telling us that realizing the Great Reset is a precursor to
sustainable development. They say it's all about the environment. As
we discussed in the energy and climate chapter, they've been saying for
fifty years that if we don't act fast, the world will end. Many of these
elites have gone so far as to say that the world will end in a cataclysmic
event, if we don't do exactly what they say!

As we discussed already, the World Economic Forum has been saying that lockdowns are quietly improving cities around the world.

Yes, millions of people are losing their jobs.

Supply chains are breaking down.

Millions are being pushed into poverty.

Suicides.

Drug overdoses.

As they say, it's actually improving the planet! Right?!

So the first thing, if you haven't caught on by now, is they want
us off of meat. They don't want us eating meat. Why? Why don't they
want us eating meat? Is it for our health?

Let's dig into that a little bit.

As mentioned, Henry Kissinger says that if you can control the food, you can control the people. The globalists say we need to go on a planetary health diet to save the world, as stated in a World Economic Forum article from 2019 with the title "Why We Need to Go On the 'Planetary Health Diet' to Save the World." Here's an excerpt from that article:

> As the below chart shows, the main change to many Western diets is going to be in the consumption of red meat, cutting back to only 14g a day (and just 30 calories), which equates to about a mouthful of a typical Sirloin steak.
>
> Starchy vegetables, including potatoes and cassava, a staple in African countries, are limited to just 50g a day, while fish, which is such a big part of Japanese and other Asian diets, is limited to 28g.[25]

Are we in the West only going to get a single mouthful of red meat a day? It seems that Japan and other Asian countries aren't going to fare much better with two mouthfuls of fish. And if you're African, it looks like you'll only get about three-and-a-half mouthfuls of potato or cassava. In their own words, what's the plan? They tell us:

> The reports says: "This includes more than doubling the consumption of healthy foods such as fruits, vegetables, legumes and nuts, and a greater than 50% reduction in global consumption of less healthy foods such as added sugars and red meat."
>
> . . . The 'planetary health diet', which involves a shift towards plant-based eating, was designed by 37 experts as part of the EAT-Lancet Commission to answer the question of how we're going to feed a projected 10 billion people, without destroying the planet by 2050.[26]

What do the globalists have against meat? It might be that eating and cooking meat is what made us the brilliant, quarreling humans we are today, as detailed in a 2016 story from *TIME* magazine, quoting a study from *Nature*:

> As a new study in *Nature* makes clear, not only did processing and eating meat come naturally to humans, it's entirely possible that without an early diet that included generous amounts of animal protein, we wouldn't have even become human-at least not the modern, verbal, intelligent humans we are . . .
>
> . . . According to Harvard University biologists Katherine Zink and Daniel Lieberman, the authors of the *Nature* paper, proto-humans eating enough root food to stay alive would have had to go through up to 15 million "chewing cycles" a year.
>
> This is where meat stepped-and ran and scurried-in to save the day. Prey that has been killed and then prepared either by slicing, pounding or flaking provides a much more calories-rich meal with much less chewing that root foods do, boosting nutrient levels overall.[27]

If it was meat that fueled our explosive growth in intelligence and ability to problem-solve, is it reasonable to ask what would happen to a modern brain deprived of meat? Would we become less intelligent? Some research, reported in the *BBC* for 2020, supports this possibility:

> Ideally, to test the impact of the vegan diet on the brain, you would take a randomly selected group of people, ask half to stop eating animal products-then see what happens. But there isn't a single study like this.
>
> Instead, the only research that comes close involved the reverse. It was conducted on 555 Kenyan schoolchildren, who were fed one of three different types of soup—one with meat, one with milk, and one with oil—or no soup at all, as a snack over seven school terms. They were tested before and after, to see how their intelligence compared. Because of their economic circumstances,

the majority of the children were de facto vegetarians at the start of the study.[28]

It's not a perfect study, but a pretty good one. The children were de facto vegetarians. Then, they were given meat and followed over seven school terms. The results should have us questioning any move toward an exclusively plant-based diet:

> Surprisingly, the children who were given the soup containing meat each day seemed to have a significant edge. By the end of the study, they outperformed all the other children on a test for non-verbal reasoning. Along with the children who received soup with added oil, they also did best on a test of arithmetic ability. Of course, more research is needed to verify if this effect is real, and if it would also apply to adults in affected countries. But it does raise some intriguing questions about whether veganism could be holding some people back.[29]

Admittedly, much of this is hypothetical, and while there doesn't seem to be a lot of good data, that doesn't seem to be stopping the globalist war on meat. Why might that be?

Meat is likely associated with higher intellectual function.

If you're lying to people, it's probably easier if they're not as smart as they might otherwise be. Some evidence suggests veganism is likely associated with lower intellectual function.

I believe a planet of vegans would be much easier to control than a planet of meat eaters.

\* \* \*

Bill Gates has become the largest owner of farmland in the United States and owns over 242,000 acres of farmland.[30]

He seems to be following in lockstep with Kissinger.

According to the latest numbers from 2021, there are approximately 895 million acres of farmland in the United States.[31] Although he is the largest owner of farmland, he still seems to own a relatively small share, less than 1 percent.

If the World Economic Forum says that you will own nothing and be happy, why is Bill Gates so busy buying all the farmland?

Could it be that you will own nothing, but they will own everything?

An article in *Forbes* in 2019 explained why money managers were moving into farmland and noted in the introductory paragraph the acquisitions of Bill Gates:

> Farmland has proven to be an attractive asset class for professional investors, with almost uniformly positive returns since the early 1990s. This is because investors can make money from two ways: from the annual cash rent that farmers pay to use the land and also from steady increases in land values.
>
> For example, consider a standard piece of farmland in the Midwest or the South. Assuming an annual cash rent of 4% and land value growth of 6%, the total return would be around 10% For stable and productive row-crop farms, this would be considered normal or even attractice long-term returns in the current environment. On the other end of the spectrum, an almond farm in California may produce an 8% yield and annual land value growth of 4%, resulting in annualized returns of 12%.[32]

It seems like in the real future the globalists have planned, you'll own nothing, Bill Gates will be your landlord, and he'll be very happy collecting all that rent.

\* \* \*

I want you to see all of this as part of a plan.

Bill Gates and big money have stepped into controlling and consolidating the farmland and food supply. The number of independent farms has gone down drastically, from 2,166,780 farms in 2000, to 2,012,050 in 2020, a loss of more than 150,000 farms.[33]

You may notice that this is the same strategy they've used in their war against businesses during lockdowns. You couldn't shop at the mom-and-pop retailers, but you could go to Target, Walmart, and Costco or order online from Amazon and put money in the pocket of Jeff Bezos?

Whether you believe it was part of a plan, or just how things happened during the lockdowns, many small retailers went out of business, leading to record profits among the large retailers, just the sort of people who attend the yearly meetings of the World Economic Forum in Davos, Switzerland. By thinning the ranks of the competitors, the globalists can much more easily pick off the few remaining survivors.

Alarmingly, the food business is controlled by just a handful of large corporations. According to an article from the Greenpeace website:

> Six corporations—Monsanto, DuPont, Dow, Syngenta, Bayer and BASF—control 75 percent of the world pesticides market.
>
> Factory farms now account for 72 percent of poultry production, 43 percent of egg production, and 55 percent of pork production worldwide.
>
> Only four corporations—ADM, Bunge, Cargill and Dreyfuss—control more than 75 percent of the global grain trade. They overwhelmingly push commodity crops like corn and soy on local farmers at the expense of native farmers.[34]

Consolidation makes it easier to control an industry, just as the Rockefeller family did in the nineteenth century with oil and gas. You see, these billionaires claim to be philanthropists, but it's the same old playbook: figure out how to create a monopoly.

And if we get rid of the farmers who raise meat products, what will we eat? Bill Gates has a couple ideas. You might want his lab-grown synthetic meat. How appetizing! Here's Bill Gates talking about it in February of 2021:

I do think all the rich countries should move to 100% synthetic beef. You can get used to the taste difference, and the claim is they're going to make it taste even better over time. Eventually, the green premium is modest enough that you can sort of change the [behavior of] people or use regulation to totally shift the demand.

So for meat in the middle-income-and-above countries, I do think it's possible. But it's one of those ones where, wow, you have to track it every year and see. And the politics are [challenging]. There are all these bills that say it's basically got to be called, basically lab garbage, to be sold. They don't want us to use the beef label.[35]

Is it just me, or is it a little creepy to have the world's wealthiest man casually talk about changing the behavior of people or using "regulation to shift the demand"? He seems to believe that these governments, which at the very least want these abominations properly labeled, are just kind of annoying.

However, if you don't like his lab-grown synthetic beef, he's got another nifty plan with Jeff Bezos of Amazon and former Vice President Al Gore:

Bill Gates, Jeff Bezos, and Al Gore are among the big names backing Nature's Fynd, a startup developing meatless burgers, dairy free cheese, chicken-less nuggets, and other products using a fermented volcanic microbe derived from Yellowstone National Park . . .

. . . Nature's Fynd was co-founded in 2012 by Thomas Jonas and Mark Kozubal, originally under the name Sustainable Bioproducts. Before cofounding the company, Kozubal had researched a microbe from volcanic hot springs in Yellowstone National Park called *Fusarium strain flavolapis.*

Kozubal and a team of scientists fermented the microbe into a protein-rich substance they called "Fy," which is now the foundation for their food products.[36]

Okay, the world is going to depend on a microbe from a volcanic hot spring for its protein needs. What could possibly go wrong with that?

They are now even promoting that we should eat bugs! But don't take my word for it. According to a CNN Health headline: "The Food that Can Feed, and Maybe Save the Planet: Bugs!" From the article:

> On a morning in the not-too-distant future, you might toast bread made with cricket flour, drink a protein smoothie made from locust powder, and eat scrambled eggs (made extra creamy with the fat from mopane caterpillars) with a side of mealworm bacon.
>
> That meal will give you four times the iron, more than three times the protein and more key vitamins and minerals than the bread, smoothie, eggs and bacon you eat today—all while saving the planet.[37]

This control of food is a classic problem, reaction, and solution.

The problem: "We need to shift to a plant-based diet!"

The reaction: "We must get rid of all the meat and give you substitutes!"

The solution: Give you lab-grown meats!

Lobby governments to enact laws to move people into fake and unhealthy meats.

People get sicker.

Big Pharma makes more money.

Oh, and if you get really hungry, you can eat bugs!

## Chapter Nine

# The Globalists Try to Find the Narrative

Schwab and his Davos buddies keep trying to come up with a storyline that motivates people more than the classical idea that individuals struggle to lead a virtuous life, and, in that effort, society is benefited.

It seems as if they believe their failure to move people is because they just haven't come up with that magical myth that the idiots will blindly follow.

Schwab first tried to pitch *The Fourth Industrial Revolution*, but it didn't catch fire.

When that failed, he released the book *Shaping the Future of the Fourth Industrial Revolution*, maybe because like a tourist in a foreign country he believes that if he just speaks slowly and loudly, he can get the locals to understand him.

Next, he tried *COVID-19: The Great Reset*, but that was also a clunker. Maybe it struck people as a little insensitive for Schwab to say in effect, "Hey, I know there was a global pandemic that killed millions of people, but let's look at this as an opportunity!"

Maybe instead of being so provocative he wanted to try for an exceptionally boring title, so his next effort, published in January 2021, was *Stakeholder Capitalism: A Global Economy that Works for Progress,*

*People and the Planet.* Let's take a closer look at this effort, cowritten with Peter Vanham, who is head of Chairman's (Klaus Schwab) Communications at the World Economic Forum. In other words, he just happened to be in the office, so to speak.

It must be so difficult for Klaus Schwab to have all of these important people praising his book, only to have the regular people treat you like an embarrassing uncle. This is from Marc Benioff, chair and CEO of Salesforce:

> Fifty years ago Klaus Schwab first proposed his theory that businesses are not only responsible to their shareholders, but also to all their stakeholders. With a global economic system generating deep divisions and inequalities, Klaus renews his call for a form of capitalism that works for everyone and where businesses don't just take from society, but truly give back and have a positive impact. *Stakeholder Capitalism* is an urgent call to action.[1]

Marc Benioff would have you believe that before Klaus Schwab, nobody had ever raised the idea that businesses should be concerned with humanity.

What kind of childhood did Benioff have?

Did his parents never allow him to watch one of the many film adaptations of *A Christmas Carol* around the holidays? Has he never seen the ghost of Jacob Marley scream at Ebenezer Scrooge that instead of being a good man of business, "Mankind was my business"? Has Marc Benioff never heard of charity?

Schwab moves onto the praise from his next good friend, Alexander De Croo, the prime minister of Belgium, who wrote:

> If you think this is just another pre-COVID/post-COVID book, think again. Klaus Schwab draws on his vast experience to take us on a roller-coaster ride past the highs and lows of post-war capitalism. His knock for economic storytelling gives you a real

and deep insight into where we are headed and what we should be aiming for.[2]

Yes, I'm sure the general public has been thinking to themselves, "I've read so many pre- and post-COVID books and how the world is going to change, by so many dictators who want to rule humanity. What is this one going to say that's new?" Unfortunately, it seems that the politicians in every country have to start off by saying the stupidest possible thing.

The prime minister of the Netherlands, Mark Rutte, doesn't fare much better. This is his contribution:

> In *Stakeholder Capitalism* my good friend Professor Schwab outlines an inspiring way forward in making the global economy more equitable, sustainable, and future proof. A vision that fits in perfectly with all his efforts over the years to build a better world. Once again, Professor Schwab gives us food for thought and reflection with this fascinating book.[3]

I find myself a little confused by the pronouncement of the prime minister of the Netherlands. How exactly is Schwab going to make the global economy "future-proof"? Does that mean no dissent will be allowed? No disruptive technologies will be released to the public? Is it just me, or does it seem like the globalists don't like any future they don't control?

In the preface, Schwab supports my premise that whether it was before COVID or after COVID, the Davos crowd has always been about globalism and tighter control over the world population. Schwab writes:

> But now, we have some distance from the initial crisis, and many of us—including myself—have come to realize the pandemic and its effects are deeply linked to problems we had already

identified with the existing global economic system. This perspective brought me back to the discussion I had been having in
February 2020 on the date of that fateful call from Beijing. Many
of the analyses we had previously been working on were more
true that ever. You will be able to read about them in this book.[4]

Don't you just love the intellectual openness of your typical globalist?
He might as well have written, *I thought I was right before the pandemic.
But now I know I'm even more right.*

No pause, no reflection, no criticism of anything that went on with
any government anywhere in the world. Of course, those evil individual people will come in for strong criticism, on account of not being
collaborative and cooperative.

But all those governments?

They're just good and pure, like fresh rainwater from the sky.

And would it be a Klaus Schwab book without unfailing praise for
the brutality of the Chinese communist party?

> Under the leadership of Chairman Mao, from 1949 to 1975, the
> Communist Party of China (CPC) became the lone governing
> party of the country, ending the political turmoil more decid-
> edly. The CPC founded the People's Republic of China as a sin-
> gle-party state, which brought stability to the regime for the price
> of democratic freedom.[5]

"Democratic freedom." Is that just a quaint little concept, like chocolate bunnies at Easter? Or could it possibly be more important? An
ideal for which people have fought and died over the centuries? Schwab
spends no time on the concept, only noting how during the time of
Chairman Mao, China did not experience much economic progress.
Instead, it was Mao's successor, Deng Xiaoping, who pursued increased
economic progress, while the state maintained an iron grip on power.
Schwab wrote:

Deng wanted to change that, and in 1978 he visited Singapore. At the time, the island city-state was one of the four so-called Asian Tigers (Hong Kong, Taiwan, Singapore, and South Korea), economies based on foreign direct investments (FDI), the shielding of key industries from foreign competition, and export-led growth. Having been inspired by the city-state's example, he pursued a new economic development model for China as well: the Reform and Opening-Up, starting in 1979.[6]

Let's be honest about some of our terms. What's meant by "the shielding of key industries from foreign competition"? That's protectionism, plain and simple.

When we talk about "foreign direct investment," what we mean is international money men who are not interested in local conditions, just the amount of profit they can make.

And how can a government promise these international financiers the maximum amount of profit? By having a one-party government, which is essentially what all of these so-called "Asian Tigers" were and remain at this writing.

This is what Schwab himself wrote of Singapore:

> In addition, Singapore's electoral model is very different from that of many other democracies. The ruling People's Action Party has led single-party governments continuously since Singapore's independence in 1965. Other parties do participate in the country's general elections, organized every five years, and in 2020 even won close to 40 percent of the vote. But these opposition parties have failed so far to win a significant number of seats or lead major government ministries. As a result, Nikkei Asian review reported, "Singapore ranked 75th in the Economist Intelligence Unit's global democracy index for 2019, behind regional peers Malaysia, (43rd), Indonesia (64th), and Thailand (68th). The city-state performed especially poorly in the category of "electoral process and pluralism."[7]

Schwab does his usual analysis, mentioning a glaring flaw, such as the fact an opposition party has not won an election in fifty-seven years in Singapore, then just moves on.

The model Schwab loves is a simple one. The power of the state is combined with the power of big business, and the people are left without a voice.

Tyrants always believe they're the smartest person in every room they occupy.

* * *

For Schwab, elections just seem to be a formality. He'll work with those who got to their positions of power through the ballot or the bullet. The important thing is that the leaders do his bidding. But in Schwab's formulation of the world, there's no doubt it's the corporations who should be in charge:

> To avoid the worst and achieve the best possible outcome, all stakeholders should remember the lessons from the past, and governments should shape inclusive policies and business practices. The challenge in regulating technological breakthrough is often the speed of innovation. As a frustrated chief executive once expressed to me: "Business moves in an elevator lifted by the force of creativity; governments and regulatory agencies take the stairs of incremental learning." This situation poses a particular responsibility to companies in ensuring that all technological advances are well understood, not only in terms of their functionality for individual users, but also what they mean for society more broadly.[8]

Schwab seems to treat the government like some elderly parent who must occasionally be instructed what's proper to say these days, and what should not be said. In Schwab's view of the world, all honor and glory must go to the businessperson or entrepreneur, with little if any consideration of the value of oversight. And as for the public? Well, the entrepreneur must make sure to talk to them like scared children who for some reason have an irrational fear of their latest offerings.

But sometimes the best spokesperson for the globalist might be an actual child, like Greta Thunberg. At the time she burst onto the world stage, and the stage at the World Economic Forum, she was only sixteen years old. I wonder if she realizes the incongruity of her being allowed to lecture, on such a stage to the wealthiest people in the world, that they have not done enough. Hopefully, at some point as she gains a few more years and some more life experience, she will more deeply question the motives of those who promoted her on their various platforms. Schwab quotes with approval part of Thunberg's speech from the World Economic Forum in Davos, Switzerland, in January 2019:

> At places like Davos, people like to tell success stories. But their financial success has come with an unthinkable price tag. And on climate change, we have to acknowledge that we have failed. All political movements in their present form have done so. And the media has failed to create broad public awareness.[9]

Schwab was quite clear in 2022 that he didn't want any dissent at his World Economic Forum. So how is it that he's promoting this young woman on his stage to criticize every member of the Davos gathering?

My answer is because it serves the goals of Klaus Schwab.

In order to take power, Schwab and his globalists need everything to be torn down. Thunberg wants to tear things down as well, so it serves his ends. Schwab continued:

> Thunberg had become known for her School Strike for Climate a few months earlier, shaking up the debate about what has become known as the global climate crisis. In Davos, she used the platform to give the world a hard wake-up call on the actions needed to avert catastrophe. "Adults keep saying: 'We owe it to the young people to give them hope,'" she said at a special press conference.

"But I don't want your hope. I don't want you the be hopeful. I want you to panic. I want you to feel the fear I feel every day. And then I want you to act. I want you to act as you would in a crisis. I want you to act as if your house is on fire. Because it is."[10]

We all remember what it was like to be young and filled with moral righteousness. But as we matured, we started to have a greater understanding of the complexity of the world. We came to understand that the best decisions are not made from a place of panic, but from calm, rational consideration. If you were trapped in a burning house, would you want the fireman coming to rescue you to be filled with panic? Or would you want a fireman, completely aware of the danger, methodically plotting out the best route to safety through the flames?

Schwab then moves on, from provoking you into a state of panic to hoping you follow his rash suggestions. In his section on "The Key Tasks of National Governments," Schwab lays it out:

At its simplest, the government's main role in the stakeholder model is to enable *equitable prosperity*. That means a government should enable any individual actor to maximize his or her *prosperity* but do so in a way that is *equitable* for both people and the planet. It should do so in three primary ways. First, a government should value the contributions everybody makes to society, provide equal opportunities to all, and curb any excessive inequalities as they arise. Second, it should act as an arbiter and regulator for companies operating in the free market. And third, as a guardian of future generations, it should put a stop to activities that degrade the environment.[11]

Let's consider all the various things wrong with Schwab's modest proposal. He seeks to change the fundamental role of government from that of protecting the rights of individuals to live as they see fit to this new goal of "equitable prosperity." I'm absolutely terrified of vague expressions like "equitable prosperity" because they can so easily be used to justify acts of injustice. Let's say we've got two kids on a baseball team, but one of them can't hit a ball to save his life, while the other keeps hitting home runs. Is it "equitable" to let one of the kids have a career in professional baseball, while the other needs to pursue a different career, like accounting?

This is comforting pablum, used to lull the public into not fully understanding the massive grab of power the globalists intend to pursue. Here's an example: "The government should value the contributions everybody makes to society."

Does that include drug dealers, murderers, war profiteers, and child molesters?

In Schwab's formulation, the government, at this point no doubt stacked with globalists, will "act as an arbiter and regulator for companies operating in the free market." Do you see how the government has just usurped the role of the justice system in Schwab's plan? And you can be certain that if the globalists are acting as regulators of the economy, there will be no "free market," just crony capitalism and monopolies for their favorite friends.

Finally, Schwab claims the government role as "a guardian of future generations" in order to protect the environment. Now, I consider myself an environmentalist, not wanting people to spray chemicals that cause the frogs to . . . well . . . behave in unusual ways, or have people eat genetically modified foods that I believe will negatively impact their health, but I'll detail for you exactly what I believe is wrong and what needs to be done to fix it. What I won't do is proclaim some universal right for the government to do anything it damned well pleases if it justifies it on the basis of environmentalism.

This is the way tyrants take power.

They don't tell you they want to steal your rights.

They tell you that if you just give them the power, they will make it all better.

But don't listen to them.

Making the world a better place, whatever you believe that to be, is your job.

* * *

Why is it that I remain so optimistic about our ability to defeat the globalists?

It's because they can't tell a story to save their lives, and stories run the world.

They fail to realize stories of freedom, of humanity's ability to triumph over great odds, are always more popular than stories of slavery, or eternally young cyborgs, sexless and nonbreeding.

We are aware of what's wrong in the world.

We want our stories to tell us how we, as individuals, can become heroes, and make use of our limited time on this planet.

Nothing proclaims the absolute failure of the globalists to say anything that the common people would support more than the publication on December 28, 2021, of Schwab's latest book (cowritten with Thierry Mallert), *The Great Narrative for a Better Future*. As Schwab himself wrote in the introduction:

> As the most effective of conduits for ideas, narratives have the unique power to help us determine what's going on, what lies ahead and what needs to be done, hence the title of this book. Defined in the simplest possible terms, a narrative is a story about something. More aptly for the purpose of The Great Narrative, it is also "a way of presenting or understanding a situation or events that reflects and promotes a particular view or set of values."[12]

The problem that Schwab never seems to consider is whether the narrative is true. What follows is Schwab's choosing of experts who reflect his point of view that the increasing complexity of the world requires greater authoritarian power, whether in direct government action or social shaming.

But he never stops to consider the fundamental lie at the heart of his narrative.

The lie is that the individual cannot be trusted to make their own decisions.

It's a lie they'll never be able to sell, no matter how many experts they get to tell you that you can't be trusted with the choices for your life.

Recently, Hollywood was rocked by the unexpected success of a movie that few expected to be so wildly popular. The star was recreating a role that he'd first played thirty-five years earlier, it dealt with genuine military heroism, and there was nothing remotely "woke" about it. I am speaking of course of Tom Cruise's movie *Top Gun: Maverick*, in which he portrays Pete "Maverick" Mitchell.

What the globalists don't seem to understand is that a narrative can be "fictional" and yet reveal an underlying truth about humanity. We cheer not for the escape from almost certain death, but because it renews our belief in humanity's potential for greatness.

The first scene sets the stage for the story that follows: Maverick is the test pilot for a futuristic jet called Dark Star, but the program is slated to be canceled in favor of unmanned drones. The essential conflict is set: Man v. the machine. Dark Star is set for a test flight that day, at which point it's supposed to go to Mach 9, which would be a world record. Eventually, the plane is expected to reach Mach 10.

But the flight has been canceled by the general (wonderfully played by Ed Harris).

Maverick talks with the flight crew, who all know their jobs are about to be canceled along with the project.

Maverick decides to take the jet up, because if he reaches Mach 9, the program must continue, as per the contract. At this point, Maverick is fighting for the jobs of his friends. Maverick takes off just as the general arrives and quickly climbs to the required altitude, all while the general is cursing out the flight crew.

But the general can't do anything because Maverick is already airborne.

Within a few minutes, Maverick has the jet up to Mach 9, and the ground crew tells him he can come back down. But Maverick has other plans. He takes the jet up to Mach 10. He has saved the jobs of the flight crew, but now he's seeing what is possible with the aircraft. The flight crew tells him to back it off, but Maverick keeps pushing. When he gets it up to Mach 10.3, the jet starts vibrating wildly, then disintegrates.

The screen is silent with us seeing a distant shot of the plane's debris falling to Earth.

Has our hero died?

The movie just started.

We do not see Maverick falling to Earth, maybe struggling to open his parachute, filled with terror.

Instead, we see the astonished flight crew, including the general, hanging their heads at what they believe to be the end of Pete "Maverick" Mitchell.

The next scene is of some cowboy diner, maybe in the Rocky Mountains, and Maverick stumbles in, dazed, wearing his flight jacket, soot on his face, his hair blown back like some fighter jock Einstein, and he asks, "Where am I?"

The diners are startled by his appearance, none of them speak, then one small boy pipes up, "Earth."

Incredibly cheesy, you might say.

But there is brilliance to the story because it mirrors what we believe in the depths of our souls. Tom Cruise gives us a vision of how we want to one day present ourselves to God.

I will fight to save those I love.

I will fight next to realize great ambitions.

And in the end, I will fight to be a completely unique individual.

The globalists will never come up with such a compelling narrative because they don't believe in humanity.

\* \* \*

An inevitable consequence of the globalists believing they know how things should be done better than you do comes across loud and clear when they try to establish cooperation. Because they're not genuinely talking about cooperation. They're talking about submission to their will.

Watch how Schwab tries first to push you into that panic stage, before moving in for the kill:

> Truly shared values and well-established moral principles such as integrity, solidarity and fairness are the glue that binds societies, enabling them to function and thrive in an atmosphere of trust. The magnitude of the issues we collectively face today (a deadly virus making us fear for our lives; the climate and environmental crisis and the degradation of nature generating existential fear about the future; the speed of technological change provoking anxiety for our livelihoods and our way of life) often shifts our attitudes from altruistic to self-centered.[13]

This is the persuasion play. Make an appeal to widely accepted values, such as "integrity, solidarity and fairness," then pivot to the fear: COVID, climate change, environmental degradation, and the pace of technological change. The reader feels a little disoriented because they've been moved so quickly from a place of pleasure (considering the values of integrity, solidarity, and fairness) to fears of the future, and then when they're in a vulnerable state, tell them they've gone from being altruistic to self-centered.

It really is domestic abuse of the reader, and you might want to seek out a shelter for reader abuse victims.

Schwab then moves into the savior role.

Isn't it strange that for five books, Schwab has revealed nothing about himself? When politicians are trying to win our vote, don't they usually tell us every nauseating detail about themselves, like what their elementary school bus ride was like or whether they may have bullied somebody in high school and live today in continual shame over the harm they may have inflicted decades ago?

I believe it's a strategy.

Schwab has made himself a blank slate, like movie stars used to do before they thought it was a good idea to share everything about themselves. That's because he knows that if he talks about the failures of others, the conclusion readers will draw is that Schwab and his Davos buddies have none of those flaws. They are consciously assuming the mantle of the Ubermenschen, the supermen, who never share the slightest detail about themselves, which would make us connect with them as human beings:

> Today this polarization is cleaving our liberal societies and is a key threat to their very survival. An effective response demands the re-establishment of trust, which in turn is only possible if political and business leaders exemplify the moral standards expected of them. Only by walking the value talk will they have the authority to implement essential value-oriented policies.[14]

I can't get over the fact that I've never once heard Schwab say his Davos buddies or government leaders need to talk to individual people. It's fine to talk to members of groups. But don't you learn so much more about people when you simply sit down and talk with them for a few hours? It's how human beings have solved problems for hundreds of thousands of years. Maybe our primitive ancestors, with no modern technology, had an exceptional advantage over us. If there was somebody within the tribe they disagreed with, they had to solve the problem. They couldn't just stalk off to their tepee and get on their iPhone to surf the Paleolithic web. People would notice unresolved conflicts, which might potentially threaten the ability of the tribe to survive in a brutal world that was often indifferent to their survival.

As I've said before, the globalists have been using every world crisis, from World War I to COVID-19, to push their agenda. Each crisis demands the same response they've been making for more than a century:

Everything that comes in the post-pandemic era will lead us to rethink the role of government. Rather than simply fixing market failures when they arise, they should, as suggested by the economist Marianna Mazzucato, "move towards actively shaping and creating markets that deliver sustainable and inclusive growth. They should also ensure that partnerships with businesses involving government funds are driven by public interest, not profit." Looking to the future, governments will most likely, but with different degrees of intensity, **decide that it's in the best interest of society to rewrite some of the rules of the game and permanently increase their role**. [Bold added by author.][15]

Again, the globalists are not interested in having a conversation with you. That's because they're smarter than you. They get to decide what's in the best interest of society, which rules need to be rewritten, and which parts of their role will be permanently increased.

And what is their goal? Schwab tells you. He thinks he has won, and yet there has never been a time in history in which the ruling powers have been more distrusted by their citizens. We are not at the end of this story. We are just at the beginning. They have operated by stealth so far, but they are coming out of the shadows. The believe they are strong. The truth is, they've never been more vulnerable:

In the US, President Biden's "Build Back Better" bill (reduced to $1.8 trillion) places the "Families Plan" and climate measures at the centerpiece of his domestic agenda and represents a major stepping stone to create a more equitable and sustainable society. In Europe, the welfare state has the reputation of being the most extensive and "generous" in the world but it might yet extend further. The level of protection varies by countries (which administer welfare policies), but the European Commission has launched a new 750 billion [Euro] "COVID-19 recovery fund" comprising four pillars, two of which are destined to reduce social and territorial inequality and to boost economic cohesion.[16]

The globalists think they're winning, but if their ideas had been any good in the first place, they wouldn't have had to conceal them.

And they still have their dissident problem, which is only going to get worse. Yes, they may kick us off their platforms, but we'll build new ones. If they demonetize us, we'll figure a way around that, as well.

Might they go so far as to kill some of us?

They might.

I don't discount that possibility.

But each death would cost them precious capital, putting the lie to their claim of doing it for the public good.

And despite all of their gun-control measures, the fact is our side has most of the guns.

The Second Amendment was not placed right after free speech because the Founding Fathers wanted to protect our right to hunt.

The Second Amendment serves as a check on a government that might seek to become a tyranny.

I understand these are scary times, but I am not afraid.

I believe, as Saint Augustine did, that "The truth is like a lion. You don't have to defend it. Let is loose. It will defend itself."[17]

I have sought to set the truth free in this book, abundantly using the words of Klaus Schwab and his fellow globalists. The power is in your hands.

However, in the final chapter of this book, I will review ten areas to watch for globalist plans, as God plans their ultimate defeat.

## Chapter Ten

# Ten Crazy Things the Globalists Say about Themselves and How to Fight Them

I think it's important to stress that in this book I have relied primarily on the writings of Klaus Schwab and other globalists like Yuval Noah Harari to justify my opinions. You may not agree with my conclusions, but I have shown my work. As Maya Angelou said, "When somebody shows you who they are, you should believe them the first time." (I am greatly indebted to Vigilant Citizen for publishing an article listing these crazy claims on *Newswars*.)[1]

\* \* \*

**The first crazy thing the globalists say is that they're penetrating world governments**. I believe I have abundantly documented their conviction that democracy is an inefficient way to run the nations of the world, and their enlightened dictatorship of scientists, engineers, and managers would do a much better job.

In a 2010 World Economic Forum report titled "Global Redesign," Schwab argued that a globalized world is best managed by a "self-selected coalition of multinational corporations, governments (including through the UN system), and select civil society organizations (CSOs)."

Schwab himself has said:

> We penetrate the cabinets. So yesterday I was at a reception for Prime Minister Trudeau and I know that half of his cabinet, or even more than half of his cabinet, are actually Young Global Leaders of the World Economic Forum . . . It's true in Argentina and it's true in France, with the President—a Young Global Leader.[2]

How are the globalists getting their way? Not by convincing the public that their plans make sense. They are doing it in secret and through stealth.

When the public discovers how they've been duped, there will come a great reckoning.

\* \* \*

**The second crazy thing the globalists believe is that they might one day use sound waves to control the behavior of people.**

In their 2018 meeting, one of the topics at the World Economic Forum was titled "Mind Control Using Sound Waves," based on an opinion piece from *Scientific American*.[3] This is from an article on the technology:

> I can see the day coming where a scientist will be able to control what a person sees in their mind's eye, by sending the right waves to the right place in their brain. My guess is that most objections will be similar to those we hear today about subliminal messages in advertisements, only much more vehement.
>
> This technology is not without its risk of misuse. It could be a revolutionary healthcare technology for the sick, or a perfect

controlling tool with which the ruthless control the weak. This time though, the control would be literal.[4]

The speaker came to the conclusion that nothing could stop this technology from being developed, but that it should be brought under the control of a benevolent organization, like the World Economic Forum, to make sure it isn't misused.

Yeah, we all know Klaus Schwab and his buddies can be trusted not to misuse a technology to control people.

\* \* \*

**The third crazy thing that globalists have said is that one day you'll take pills containing microchips.** At their 2018 World Economic Forum, there was a talk from Albert Bourla, the CEO of Pfizer, about the possibility. Here's what he said:

> FDA approved the first 'electronic pill', if I can call it that. It is basically a biological chip that is in the tablet and, once you take the tablet, and it dissolves into your stomach, it sends a signal that you took the tablet. So imagine the applications of that, the compliance. The insurance companies would know that the medicines the patients should take, they do take them. It is fascinating what happens in this field.[5]

It's interesting that these globalists never seek to engage the public in their plans. It's all about control and compliance. Whatever your age, the globalists just want to remain your eternal parent, and if you do not obey, they may just lock you in your room, no food, no water, no communication with the outside world, until you do.

\* \* \*

**The fourth crazy thing the globalists do is to praise the massive COVID lockdowns**. In fact, they praise lockdowns so much that they hate to delete some of their praise.

The World Economic Forum released a video that stated, "Lockdowns significantly reduced human activity . . . leading to Earth's quietest period in decades," at the same time they showed pictures of empty cities and closed businesses. As the video continued, they considered the lockdowns worth it because "carbon emissions were down 7% in 2020."[6]

However, because of the public outcry, the World Economic Forum had to delete the tweet that contained the video. They wrote another tweet, "We're deleting this tweet. Lockdowns aren't 'quietly improving cities' around the world. But they are an important part of the public health response to COVID-19."[7]

The COVID-19 crisis was something the globalists used because it allowed them to accelerate their plans. The problem is that it ran into massive opposition from the public, many of whom have made the ultimate decision in their mind that they will never be quiet again.

* * *

**The fifth crazy thing the globalists say is that they want to make the COVID-19 lockdowns permanent**. In a video release from August 17, 2021, they detailed all the permanent changes COVID-19 is going to bring to our lives, such as permanent masking, Purell dispensers being a ubiquitous part of your daily life, and children being stuck permanently at home, being schooled through their computer screens. In the video, they highlighted yet another cutting-edge technology: "NASA has invented a system that can ID you from your heartbeat using a laser."[8]

What better way to control people than by telling them they have to fear an invisible enemy and must remain forever locked in their homes and cowering in fear from it?

Beware of tyrants who tell you to live in a permanent state of fear.

\* \* \*

**The sixth crazy thing the globalists do is to crow their undisguised delight that the COVID-19 crisis might allow them to speed up their plans for the Great Reset.** In a video they released in 2021 on the Great Reset, they managed to confirm all of the worst fears people had about them.[9]

In one image, they show a tombstone with the words "Capitalism R.I.P. 2020," and near the end the narrator puts it plainly: "And that's all about getting the right people in the right place at the right time." This is not the organic growth of the marketplace, nor an arena in which the best ideas and products become the most popular.

The globalists are looking to kill classic capitalism and replace it with crony capitalism.

\* \* \*

**The seventh crazy thing the globalists want to do is get rid of freedom of speech, which they define as the "recalibration of speech."** This was stated most clearly in a speech by Australian eSafety Commissioner Julie Inman Grant, from the Davos Conference of May 2022. She said:

> We are finding ourselves in a place where we have increasing polarization everywhere and everything feels binary when it doesn't need to be. So I think we're going have to think about a recalibration of a whole range of human rights that are playing out online. You know, from freedom of speech to the freedom to be free from online violence.[10]

How can we understand this other than as a call for changing freedom of speech? As I believe it, free speech itself is binary.

We either have it or we don't.

* * *

**The eighth crazy thing the globalists say is that the World Economic Forum wants to put chips in your clothing.** They released a video on the idea in 2022.[11]

These chips would function as digital passports, and also allow fashion brands to resell their clothes. Imagine the possibilities for tracking you. According to the video, these products are coming out in 2025 from Microsoft.

I'm not going to be wearing any.

* * *

**The ninth crazy thing the globalists say is that the World Economic Forum is promoting the possibility of implanting smartphones into your body by 2030.** Think about that. It's not enough that it's always in your hand anyway. They published a video on the possibility in 2022.[12]

This feeds into the interest by the World Economic Forum for transhumanism, or as Yuval Noah Harari stated, making you an "eternally young cyborg, sexless and nonbreeding."

Doesn't that sound exciting?

A future with no sex, no kids, and a smartphone implanted in your body.

* * *

**The tenth crazy thing the globalists do is how freely they state that in the future you will own nothing and be happy.** In 2016, Ida Auken, a member of Parliament in Denmark, said it very clearly: "Welcome to 2030. I own nothing, have no privacy, and life has never been better." The World Economic Forum loved that formulation so much that they tweeted about it on December 27, 2016.[13]

The World Economic Forum even put out an article titled "8 Predictions for the World in 2030," with that phrase, "You'll own nothing and be happy."

The article explained:

> "I don't own anything. I don't own a car. I don't own a house. I don't own any appliances or any clothes," writes Danish MP Ida Auken. Shopping is a distant memory in the city of 2030, whose inhabitants have cracked clean energy and borrow what they needed on demand. It sounds utopian, until she mentions that her every move is tracked and outside the city live swathes of discontents, the ultimate vision of a society split in two.[14]

And there we have it. The ultimate outcome of the plan of the globalists. We will have a visible split between the slaves and the free people. The elite will struggle to give all the benefits to the members of their city and try to starve those who live outside the city.

Now we know what happens to the dissidents.

They will be exiled, kept from the city, and forced into a digital gulag.

\* \* \*

How do we fight back against this darkness?

By bringing their plans into the light. Shed light on the lies when you see them. Write a letter to the editor, call up talk radio shows, and use your online abilities to make your voice heard.

The Gospel of John gives me comfort when it says, "The light shines in the darkness, and the darkness has not overcome it."[15]

It really is that simple. When we shine the light on darkness, the darkness cannot fight back. It can only retreat. In this book, I hope I've been shining a powerful light on this globalist darkness. I'm not saying it's going to be easy.

But it is what they fear.

I think when one reads their writings it becomes crystal clear how much they fear the public.

It is why they lie to you.

For more than a century, the globalists have been afraid to tell you the truth.

As their plans materialize, do you think the common people are simply going to say, "Wow, I'm glad you didn't tell me all of this before, but now that it's here, I love it!"?

The reason they didn't tell people about their plans is they knew you would hate it.

However, when they spring the truth on people, they'll still hate it just as much as if they'd been told about it all along.

We are in a war for the future of the world. The globalists want an antihuman future in which they will capture control of our species and direct the future of human development. But that's not a future the people want. They want a future of freedom, where scientific discoveries liberate them to be so much more than they could ever be when they were focused on mere survival or dealing with the ravages of disease.

When I say we are all children of God, I mean it from the viewpoint that each one of us has our own individual truth, and we seek to live according to that truth.

When a person is calm and their needs are met, they are concerned about the greater human family. Science can serve as a handmaiden of humanity's development, but it makes a poor master, which is exactly what the globalists seek to bring about.

The globalists are destined to fail.

It is God's will.

We were created to be the masters of our own fate.

We only need to choose that path, and it will open up before us.

# Notes

## Epigraph Page

[1] Ida Auken, "Welcome to 2030: I Own Nothing, Have No Privacy, and Life Has Never Been Better," November 12, 2016, *Forbes*, www .forbes.com/sites/worldeconomicforum/2016/11/10/shopping-i -cant-really-remember-what-that-is-or-how-differently-well-live -in-2030.

## Chapter One

[1] *New American Bible*, Book of Samuel, Chap. 8, 1–18 (Nashville, Tennessee, Thomas Nelson, Inc., 1987), pp. 249–250.

[2] Klaus Schwab, *The Fourth Industrial Revolution* (London, England, Portfolio/Penguin, 2016), p. vii.

[3] Ibid. at p. viii.

[4] Ibid. at p. 1.

[5] Ibid. at pp. 1–2.

[6] Ibid. at p. 2.

[7] Ibid. at p. 4.

## Chapter Two

[1] Klaus Schwab, *Shaping the Future of the Fourth Industrial Revolution* (New York, New York, Currency, 2018), p vii.

2   Ibid.

3   Ibid.

4   Ibid. at p. viii.

5   Malcom Gladwell, *Outliers: The Story of Success* (New York, New York, Back Bay Books, Little Brown and Company, 2008), p. 6.

6   Ibid. at p. 9.

7   Klaus Schwab, *Shaping the Future of the Fourth Industrial Revolution* (New York, New York, Currency, 2018), p vii.

8   Ibid. at p. ix.

9   Ibid. at p. x.

10  Ibid.

11  Ibid. at p. 3.

12  Ibid. at p. 7.

13  Ibid. at p. 14.

14  Ibid. at p. 17.

15  Ibid. at p. 19.

16  Ibid. at p. 31.

17  Ibid.

18  Ibid. at p. 33.

19  Ibid. at p. 65.

20  Jason Fernandez, "What is a Stakeholder?" *Investopedia*, August 19, 2021, www.investopedia.com/terms/s/stakeholder.asp.

21  Klaus Schwab, *Shaping the Future of the Fourth Industrial Revolution* (New York, New York, Currency, 2018), p. 79.

22  Ibid. at pp. 224–225.

23  Ibid. at p. 226

24  Ibid. at p. 230.

25  Ibid. at p. 231.

## Chapter Three

1   Patrick Wood, *Technocracy Rising* (Mesa, Arizona, Coherent Publishing, 2016), p. 49.

2   Ibid. at p. 12.

3   Thorstein Veblen, *Engineers and the Price System* (New York, New York, BW Huebsch, 1921), pp. 120–121.

4   Patrick Wood, *Technocracy Rising* (Mesa, Arizona, Coherent Publishing, 2016), p. 22.

5   Ibid. at p. 30.

6   Ibid. at p. 46.

7   Ibid. at p. 45.

8   Telephone Interview with Patrick Wood, May 4, 2022.

9   Ibid.

10  Ibid.

11  "Zbigniew Brzezinski Meeting with Deng Xiaoping, May 21, 1978," University of Southern California – Annenberg School, U.S. China Institute (accessed May 12, 2020), www.china.usc.edu/zbigniew -brzezinski-meeting-deng-xiaoping-may-21-1978.

12  Chen Weihua, "Brzezinski and His Insightful Wisdom Will Be Missed," June 6, 2017, *China Daily*, www.chinadaily.com.cn /opinion/2017-06/03/content_29601876.htm.

13  Telephone Interview with Patrick Wood, May 4, 2022.

14  Ibid.

15  Chris Cillizza, "And then Henry Kissinger Walks In . . . 24 Hours in the Donald Trump Circus," *CNN*, May 11, 2017.

16  Telephone Interview with Patrick Wood, May 4, 2022.

17  Ibid.

18  Ibid.

19  Ibid.

20  Ibid.

21  David Rockefeller, *Memoirs* (New York, New York, Random House, 2002), p. 405.

22  Ibid.

23  Ibid. at p. 415.

24  Ibid. at p. 416.

25  Ibid. at p. 417.

26  Ibid.

27  Ibid. at pp. 417–418.

28 Ibid at p. 418.

29 Ibid.

30 Zbigniew Brzezinski, *Between Two Ages: America's Role in the Technetronic Era* (Westport, Connecticut, Greenwood Press, 1970), p. 1.

31 Ibid. at pp. 199–200.

32 Ibid. at p. 200.

33 Ibid. at pp. 200–201.

34 Ibid. at p. 215.

35 Ibid. at p. 216.

36 Ibid. at pp. 252–253.

37 Ibid. at p. 260.

38 Ibid. at p. 308.

39 Martin Tolchin, "How Johnson Won Election He'd Lost," February 11, 1990, *New York Times*, www.nytimes.com/1990/02/11/us/how-johnson-won-election-he-d-lost.html.

40 Daniel Ellsberg, "Lying About Vietnam," June 29, 2001, *New York Times*, www.nytimes.com/2001/06/29/opinion/lying-about-vietnam.html.

41 B. Drummond Ayres, Jr., "Goldwater is Honored as a Man of Principle," June 4, 1998, *New York Times*, www.nytimes.com/2001/06/29/opinion/lying-about-vietnam.html.

42 Barry Goldwater, *With No Apologies: The Personal and Political Memoirs of United States Senator Barry M. Goldwater* (New York, New York, William Morrow & Company, 1979), p. 284.

43 Ibid.

44 Ibid.

45 Ibid. at p. 285.

## Chapter Four

1 "Event 201," Johns Hopkins Center for Health Security (accessed May 20, 2022), www.centerforhealthsecurity.org/event201/.

2  Declan Butler, "Engineered Bat Virus Stirs Debate Over Risky Research," *Nature Medicine*, November 12, 2015, www.nature.com /articles/nature.2015.18787.pdf.

3  Ibid.

4  Samuel Chamberlain, Mark Moore, and Bruce Golding, "Fauci Was Warned that COVID-19 May Have Been 'Engineered,' Emails Show," June 2, 2021, *New York Post*, www.nypost.com/2021/06/02/fauci-was -warned-that-covid-may-have-been-engineered-emails/.

5  The Editorial Board, "How Fauci and Collins Shut Down COVID Debate," December 21, 2021, *Wall Street Journal*, www.wsj.com/ articles/fauci-collins-emails-great-barrington-declaration-covid -pandemic-lockdown-11640129116.

6  Ibid.

7  Ibid.

8  Ibid.

9  Klaus Schwab and Terry Mallert, *COVID-19: The Great Reset* (Geneva, Switzerland, Forum Publishing, a division of the World Economic Forum, July 9, 2020), p. 12.

10  Ibid. at p. 89.

11  Ibid. at p. 105.

12  Ibid. at p. 115.

13  Ibid. at p. 123.

14  Ibid. at p. 145.

15  Ibid. at p. 167.

16  Yuval Noah Harari, "The World After Coronavirus," March 20, 2020, *Financial Times*, www.ft.com/content/19d90308-6858-11ea -a3c9-1fe6fedcca75.

17  Klaus Schwab and Terry Mallert, *COVID-19: The Great Reset* (Geneva, Switzerland, Forum Publishing, a division of the World Economic Forum, July 9, 2020), pp. 182–183.

18  Ibid. at p. 186.

19  Ibid. at p. 215.

20  Ibid. at p. 244.

21  Ibid. at p. 248.

22  Ibid. at p. 250.

23  David Walsh, "Davos 2022: What to Expect from the World Economic Forum's Most Consequential Meeting in 50 Years," May 23, 2022, *Euronews*, www.euronews.com/next/2022/05/22/davos -2022-what-to-expect-from-the-world-economic-forum-s-most -consequential-meeting-in-50.

24  Simon Kent, "Eve of Destruction: Klaus Schwab Pledges the World Can Find Salvation at Davos 2022," May 19, 2022, *Breitbart*, www.breitbart.com/politics/2022/05/19/eve-of-destruction-klaus -schwab-pledges-the-world-can-find-salvation-at-davos-2022/.

25  Ibid.

26  Joshua Klein, "Australia's eSafety Commissioner Calls for 'Recalibration' of Human Rights, Free Speech," May 24, 2022, *Breitbart*, www.breitbart.com/politics/2022/05/24/world-economic-forum -australias-esafety-commissioner-calls-for-recalibration-of-human -rights-free-speech/amp/.

27  Kurt Zindulka, "'Watch: World Economic Forum Police' Detain American Conservative Journalist Jack Posobiec at Davos," May 24, 2022, *Breitbart*, www.breitbart.com/europe/2022/05/24/watch-world -economic-forum-police-detain-american-conservative-journalist-jack -posobiec/amp/.

28  Dan Reilly, "YouTube CEO Susan Wojciki Weighs in on Misinformation at Davos," May 24, 2022, *Fortune*, www. fortune.com/2022/05/24/youtube-ceo-susan-wojcicki-world -economic-forum-davos/.

29  Ibid.

30  Kurt Zindulka, "Green Social Credit: 'Individual Carbon Footprint Tracker' Pushed by China's Alibaba at World Economic Forum," May 24, 2022, *Breitbart*, www.breitbart.com/europe/2022/05/24 /wef-individual-carbon-footprint-tracker-pushed-by-chinas-alibaba -at-davos/amp/.

31  Brian Chappata, "Soros Warns 'Civilization May Not Survive' Putin's War," May 24, 2022, *Bloomberg*, www.bloomberg.com

/news/articles/2022-05-24/george-soros-warns-civilization-may -not-survive-putin-s-war.

32  Ibid.

33  Mustafa Alrawi, "Davos 2022: Bill Gates says Pfizer Partnership Will Support Malaria mRNA Vaccine 'Dream,'" May 25, 2022, *The National News*, www.thenationalnews.com/business/2022/05/25/davos-2022 -bill-gates-says-pfizer-partnership-will-support-malaria-mrna-vaccine -dream/.

34  Simon Kent, "Watch – Klaus Schwab Lauds Davos Elites: 'The Future is Built by Us,'" May 24, 2022, *Breitbart*, www.breitbart .com/europe/2022/05/24/watch-klaus-schwab-lauds-davos-elites -the-future-is-built-by-us/.

## Chapter Five

1   Telephone Interview with Patrick Wood, May 4, 2022.

2   Leo Hohmann, "Who Influences the Influencers? Meet Klaus Schwab's Top Adviser," March 15, 2022, Leo Hohmann, www.leohohmann .com/2022/03/15/who-influences-the-influencers-meet-klaus -schwabs-chief-adviser/.

3   "Yuval Noah Harari," World Economic Forum (accessed May 25, 2022), www.weforum.org/people/yuval-noah-harari.

4   Yuval Noah Harari, *Sapiens: A Brief History of Humankind* (London, England, Vintage, Penguin, Random House, 2011), pp. 114–115.

5   Ibid. at p. 115.

6   Ibid. at p. 121.

7   Ibid. at p. 122.

8   Ibid. at p. 123.

9   Ibid.

10  Ibid. at p. 125.

11  Ibid. at p. 127.

12  Ibid. at p. 146.

13  Ibid. at p. 191.

14  Ibid. at p. 209.

15  Ibid. at p. 214.

16  Ibid. at p. 227.

17  Ibid. at pp. 231–232.

18  Ibid. at p. 422.

19  Ibid. at p. 428.

20  Ibid.

21  Ibid. at pp. 433–434.

22  Ibid. at p. 436.

23  Ibid. at p. 447.

24  Ibid.

25  Ibid. at p. 448.

26  Ibid.

27  Ibid. at pp. 450–451.

28  Ibid. at p. 453.

29  Ibid. at pp. 453–454.

30  Ibid. at p. 457.

31  Ibid. at p. 458.

32  Ibid. at p. 461.

33  Ibid. at p. 466.

34  Yuval Noah Harari, *Homo Deus: A Brief History of Tomorrow* (London, England, Penguin Random House, 2016), p. 327.

35  Ibid. at p. 329.

36  Ibid. at p. 355.

37  Ibid. at p. 356.

38  Ibid. at p. 403.

39  Ibid. at p. 409.

40  Ibid. at p. 462.

41  Yuval Noah Harari, *21 Lessons for the 21st Century* (New York, New York, Random House, 2018), p. 249.

42  Ibid. at pp. 257–258.

43  Ibid. at p. 259.

44  Ibid. at pp. 325–326.

45  Ibid. at p. 328.

[46] Ibid. at p. 329.

[47] Ibid. at p. 332.

## Chapter Six

[1] Eamon Barret, "Pepper Spray, Tow Trucks, and Bitcoin Seizures: How Canada Finally Ended the Weeks-Long Freedom Convoy Protests in Ottawa," *Fortune*, February 21, 2022, www.fortune .com/2022/02/21/canada-ottawa-freedom-convoy-protest-ends -truckers-arrest-covid-vaccine-mandate/.

[2] Ibid.

[3] Ibid.

[4] Ibid.

[5] Anugraha Sundaravelu, "Russians Cut Off from Apple Pay and Google Pay," *Metro News*, February 28, 2022, www.metro.co .uk/2022/02/28/russians-cut-off-from-apple-pay-and-google-pay -16187728/.

[6] Jeff Cox, "Fed Releases Long-Awaited Study on a Digital Dollar, But Doesn't Take a Position Yet on Creating One," January 20, 2022, *CNBC*, www.cnbc.com/2022/01/20/fed-releases-long-awaited-study-on-a -digital-dollar-but-doesnt-take-a-position-yet-on-creating-one.html.

[7] Arjun Kharpal, "China is Pushing for Broader Use of Its Digital Currency," January 10, 2022, *CNBC*, www.cnbc.com/2022/01/11 /china-digital-yuan-pboc-to-expand-e-cny-use-but-challenges-remain .html.

[8] Roman Tymotsko, "Zelenskyy Administration Launches 'State in a Smartphone' App," February 14, 2020, *The Ukrainian Weekly*, www .ukrweekly.com/uwwp/zelenskyy-administration-launches-state-in -a-smartphone-app/.

[9] Mykhailo Fedorov, "World Economic Forum – Biography" (accessed June 7, 2022), www.weforum.org/people/mykhailo-fedorov.

[10] Tim Hinchliffe, "The Fourth Industrial Revolution & the Great Reset: Programming People Like CBDCs with Digital ID," April 11, 2022, *The Sociable*, www.sociable.co/government-and

-policy/fourth-industrial-revolution-the-great-reset-programming
-people-cbdc-digital-id/.

11  Katie Canales, "China's Social Credit System Ranks Citizens and
Punishes Them with Throttled Internet Speeds and Flight Bans if
the Communist Party Deems Them Untrustworthy," December
24, 2021, *Business Insider*, www.businessinsider.com/china-social
-credit-system-punishments-and-rewards-explained-2018-4.

12  Alexandra Ma, "China reportedly Made an App to Show people if
they're Standing Near Someone in Debt – A New part of Its Intrusive
'Social Credit' Policy," January 22, 2019, *Business Insider*, www
.businessinsider.com/china-app-shows-map-of-people-in-debt-for
-social-credit-system-report-2019-1.

13  Lorrie Goldstein, "Trudeau Said he Admired China's Dictatorship
– Believe Him!", February 17, 2021, *Toronto Sun*, www.torontosun
.com/opinion/columnists/goldstein-trudeau-said-he-admired
-chinas-dictatorship-believe-him.

14  "Benjamin Teitelbaum and David Sacks," *The Glenn Beck Program*,
February 23, 2022, www.play.acast.com/s/theglennbeckprogram
/16be1784-94cb-11ec-ac18-43ea7c3f64af.

15  Ibid.

16  Ibid.

17  Didi Rankovic, "Canada's Finance Intelligence Expert Admits
Freedom Convoy Donos Posed No Threat," March 2, 2022, *Newswars*,
www.newswars.com/canadas-finance-intelligence-expert-admits
-freedom-convoy-donors-posed-no-threat/.

18  Mike Blanchfield, "Trudeau Says Canada Will Always Defend Right
to Peaceful Protest after India Criticizes PM's Farmer Remarks,"
December 4, 2020, *The Globe and Mail*, www.theglobeandmail
.com/world/article-india-formally-protests-to-canada-over
-trudeau-remarks-on-farm-2/.

19  "Summary of Terrorism Threat to the U.S. Homeland," National
Terrorism Advisory System Bulleting, U.S. Department of Homeland
Security, February 7, 2022, www.dhs.gov/ntas/advisory/national
-terrorism-advisory-system-bulletin-february-07-2022.

[20] "Summary of Terrorism Threat to the U.S. Homeland," National Terrorism Advisory System Bulleting, U.S. Department of Homeland Security, August 13, 2021, www.dhs.gov/ntas/advisory /national-terrorism-advisory-system-bulletin-august-13-2021.

[21] "Advancing Digital Agency – The Power of Data Intermediaries," World Economic Forum, February 2022, p. 24, www3.weforum .org/docs/WEF_Advancing_towards_Digital_Agency_2022.pdf.

[22] "Klaus Schwab Brags Vladamir Putin, Tony Blair, and Angela Merkel Belonged to WEF's Young Global Leaders," February 25, 2022, *YouTube*, www.youtube.com/watch?v=Vq6YaQNG05c.

[23] "Digital Identity in response to COVID-19," Digital Identity Working Group, 2022, p. 3, www.tech.gov.sg/files/media/corporate -publications/FY2021/dgx_2021_digital_identity_in_response_to _covid-19.pdf.

[24] Ibid.

[25] Ibid. at p. 17.

[26] United Nations ID 2020 (accessed June 7, 2022), www.id2020. org/.

[27] World Bank's ID4D Initiative (accessed June 7, 2022), www.id4d .worldbank.org/about-us.

[28] "Reimagining Digital Identity: A Strategic Imperative," World Economic Forum (accessed June 7, 2022), www3.weforum.org /docs/WEF_Digital_Identity_Strategic_Imperative.pdf.

[29] Isabella Chase and Rick McDonell, "The U.S. Pandemic Recovery is a Chance to Improve Digital ID," *American Banker,* May 24, 2021, www.rusi.org/explore-our-research/research-groups/centre-for -financial-crime-and-security-studies.

## Chapter Seven

[1] Catherine Clifford, "California Governor Gavin Newsom Offers Hope for State's Last Nuclear Power Plant, But Major Hurdles Remain," April 25, 2022, *CNBC*, www.cnbc.com/2022/04/29

/newsom-offers-hope-for-californias-last-nuclear-plant-diablo
-canyon.html.

2   Ibid.

3   Dale Kasler, "California Warns of Summer Blackouts Amid Heat, Drought, Climate Woes," *Sacramento Bee,* May 6, 2022, www.sacbee .com/news/california/water-and-drought/article261179737.html.

4   Sammy Roth, "California Blackouts Caused by Climate Change, Poor Planning," *Los Angeles Times,* October 6, 2020, www.latimes .com/environment/story/2020-10-06/california-rolling-blackouts -climate-change-poor-planning.

5   Karla Adam, "Boris Johnson Tells World Leaders to 'Grow Up' on Climate Change, Takes Aim at Kermit the Frog," *Washington Post,* September 23, 2021, www.washingtonpost.com/world/boris-johnson -un-cop26/2021/09/23/24d21ee4-1c4c-11ec-bea8-308ea134594f _story.html.

6   Ibid.

7   Nina Chestney, "Explainer: Why Europe Faces Climbing Energy Bills," February 3, 2022, *Reuters,* www.reuters.com/business/energy /why-europe-faces-climbing-energy-bills-2022-02-03/.

8   Anna Cooban, "UK Household Energy Bills Set to Rise by Another 40%," May 24, 2022, *CNN,* www.cnn.com/2022/05/24/energy /uk-energy-price-cap-rise-october/index.html.

9   Ibid.

10   "Poorest Face Food Crisis Amid Fertilizer Shortage," November 26, 2021, *BBC,* www.bbc.com/news/business-59428406.

11   Elon Musk, Twitter, March 4, 2022, www.twitter.com/elonmusk/status /1499907549746937860.

12   Mark Mills, "The 'New Energy Economy': An Exercise in Magical Thinking," March 2019, Manhattan Institute, p. 12, www.media4. manhattan-institute.org/sites/default/files/R-0319-MM.pdf.

13   Ibid. at p. 3.

14   Steve Symes, "New law Will Install kill Switches in All new Cars," January 5, 2022, *Yahoo News,* www.yahoo.com/now/law-install-kill -switches-cars-170000930.html.

15 "H.R. 3684, Infrastructure Investment and Jobs Act, U.S. Congress, Signed into law November 15, 2021," www.congress.gov/bill/117th -congress/house-bill/3684/text.

16 Dean Praetorius, "Could a Small Nuclear War Reverse Global Warming?", May 25, 2011, *Huffington Post*, www.huffpost.com /entry/nuclear-war-global-warming_n_828496.

17 Jessica Chasmar, "John Kerry: Ukraine Crisis is Bad, But 'Wait Until You See' Flood of Climate Refugees," March 9, 2022, *Fox News*, www.foxnews.com/politics/john-kerry-ukraine-crisis-climate -refugees.

18 Ursula von der Leyen, *Twitter*, January 20, 2022, 5:45 a.m., www .twitter.com/vonderleyen/status/1484160210277224450?lang=en.

19 Chloe Taylor, "World Leaders Outline Climate Commitments at COP26 Summit," November 1, 2021, *CNBC*, www.cnbc.com/2021 /11/01/cop26-follow-live-as-world-leaders-meet-in-glasgow-for -climate-summit.html.

20 Ibid.

21 Tucker Carlson, "Tucker: Scientists Are Pushing Human Engineering,'" *Fox News*, June 23, 2021, www.foxnews.com/transcript/tucker-scientists -are-pushing-human-engineering.

22 Ibid.

23 Ibid.

24 Rahm Emanuel, "Good-Reads quote" (accessed June 8, 2022), www.goodreads.com/quotes/717228-you-never-want-a-serious -crisis-to-go-to-waste.

25 David Harsanyi, "Get Ready for the Left's Climate-Change 'Emergency' Lockdowns," September 12, 2021, *New York Post*, www .nypost.com/2021/09/12/get-ready-for-climate-change-emergency -lockdowns/.

26 Fiona Harvey, "Equivalent of COVID Emissions Drop Needed Every Two Years – Study," March 3, 2021, *The Guardian*, www.theguardian. com/environment/2021/mar/03/global-lockdown-every-two -years-needed-to-meet-paris-co2-goals-study.

[27] Carlie Porterfield, "Report: World Needs Equivalent of Pandemic Lockdown Every Two Years to Meet Paris Carbon Emission Goals," March 3, 2022, *Forbes*, www.forbes.com/sites /carlieporterfield/2021/03/03/report-world-needs-equivalent-of -pandemic-lockdown-every-two-years-to-meet-paris-carbon-emission -goals/?sh=279bf986deed.

[28] Jim Hagemann Snabe, "The Great Acceleration: What We Need to Do to Tackle Climate Change," January 17, 2022, *World Economic Forum*, www.weforum.org/agenda/2022/01/combat-climate-change-we -need-the-great-acceleration/.

[29] Rebecca Heilweil, "Everything You Need to Know About Vaccine Passports," March 31, 2021, *Vox*, www.vox.com/recode/22349266/ vaccine-passports-vaccination-record-commpass-walmart-walgreens.

[30] "Tracking Humans: Medical Pills with MicroChips and a New Proposal to Monitor Your Carbon Footprint," May 26, 2022, *CBN News*, www1.cbn.com/cbnnews/world/2022/may/tracking -humans-medical-pills-with-microchips-and-a-new-proposal-to -monitor-your-carbon-footprint.

## Chapter Eight

[1] Meagan Vasquez and Sam Fossum, "Biden Blames Russia's War in Ukraine for Food Supply Shortages and Price Hikes," May 11, 2022, *CNN*, www.cnn.com/2022/05/11/politics/biden-food-supply-russia -ukraine/index.html.

[2] "Moldovan Government Moves to Prevent Food Shortages and Price Hikes," March 1, 2022, *BNE Intellinews*, www.intellinews.com /moldovan-government-moves-to-prevent-food-shortages-and -price-hikes-236379/.

[3] "Hungary to Ban All Grain Exports Effective Immediately – Agriculture Minister," March 4, 2022, *Reuters*, www.reuters.com /article/ukraine-crisis-hungary-grains-idAFL5N2V75IT.

[4] Pavel Polityuk and Silvia Alosi, "Explainer: UN Plan to get Ukraine Grains Out Faces Hurdles," May 24, 2022, *Reuters*, www.reuters

.com/markets/commodities/ukraine-looks-ways-get-its-grain-out
-2022-05-24/.

5   "Commission Holds First Meeting of the European Food Security Crisis
    Preparedness and Response Mechanism," March 10, 2022, *EuroReporter*,
    www.eureporter.co/politics/european-commission/2022
    /03/10/commission-holds-first-meeting-of-the-european-food-security
    -crisis-preparedness-and-response-mechanism/.

6   Melanie Risdon, "Exclusive: Food Shortages Magnified by String of
    Destroyed Food Processing Facilities," April 23, 2022, *Western Standard
    Online*, www.westernstandard.news/news/exclusive-food-shortages
    -magnified-by-string-of-destroyed-food-processing-facilities
    /article_c5e4d4c3-325f-56b4-9089-8b8a69fe7d1f.html.

7   Ibid.

8   Ibid.

9   Ibid.

10  Ibid.

11  Ibid.

12  Matt Egan, "Gas Prices Hit Yet Another Record High," May 30, 2022,
    *CNN*, www.cnn.com/2022/05/30/business/gas-prices-memorial-day
    /index.html.

13  "Drought in the Western United States," June 13, 2022, United
    States Department of Agriculture, Economic Research Service, www
    .ers.usda.gov/newsroom/trending-topics/drought-in-the-western
    -united-states/.

14  Margaret Osborne, "Officials Will Release Less Water into Lake
    Mead Because of Drought," May 5, 2022, Smithsonian, www
    .smithsonianmag.com/smart-news/officials-will-release-less-water
    -into-lake-mead-because-of-drought-180980030/.

15  Ryan Johnson, "I'm a Twenty Year Truck Driver, I Will Tell You
    Why America's 'Shipping Crisis' Will Not End," October 26, 2021,
    *Medium*, www.medium.com/@ryan79z28/im-a-twenty-year-truck
    -driver-i-will-tell-you-why-america-s-shipping-crisis-will-not-end
    -bbe0ebac6a91.

[16] Ibid.

[17] Ibid.

[18] Ibid.

[19] Ibid.

[20] Henry Kissinger, "Quote Fancy" (accessed June 8, 2022), www
.quotefancy.com/quote/1275693/Henry-Kissinger-Who-controls
-the-food-supply-controls-the-people-who-controls-the-energy.

[21] Jessica Chasmar, "John Kerry: Ukraine Crisis is Bad, But 'Wait
Until You See' Flood of Climate Refugees," March 9, 2022, *Fox
News*, www.foxnews.com/politics/john-kerry-ukraine-crisis-climate
-refugees.

[22] Tucker Carlson Tonight, "Tucker – Biden Didn't Address This,"
March 2, 2022, *Fox News*, www.foxnews.com/transcript/tucker
-biden-didnt-address-this.

[23] Ibid.

[24] Ibid.

[25] Kate Whitting, "Why We All Need to Go On the 'Planetary Health
Diet' to Save the World," January 17, 2019, World Economic Forum,
www.weforum.org/agenda/2019/01/why-we-all-need-to-go-on-the
-planetary-health-diet-to-save-the-world/.

[26] Ibid.

[27] Jeffrey Kluger, "Sorry Vegans: Here's How Meat-Eating Made Us
Human," March 9, 2016, *Time*, www.time.com/4252373/meat
-eating-veganism-evolution/.

[28] Zaria Gorvett, "How a Vegan Diet Could Affect Your Intelligence,"
January 27, 2020, *BBC*, www.bbc.com/future/article/20200127
-how-a-vegan-diet-could-affect-your-intelligence.

[29] Ibid.

[30] Noah Manskar, "Bill Gates is Reportedly the Largest Farmland
Owner in America," January 15, 2021, *New York Post*, www.nypost
.com/2021/01/15/bill-gates-is-the-largest-farmland-owner-in
-america-report/

[31] "Total Area of Land in Farmland," March 14, 2021, Statista, www
.statista.com/statistics/196104/total-area-of-land-in-farms-in-the
-us-since-2000/.

[32] Carter Mallory, "Why Money Managers are Moving Into Farmland,"
July 9, 2019, Forbes, www.forbes.com/sites/forbesfinancecouncil
/2019/07/09/why-money-managers-are-moving-into-farmland/.

[33] "Total Number of Farms in the United States from 2000 to 2020,"
Statista, March 14, 2022, www.statista.com/statistics/196103/number
-of-farms-in-the-us-since-2000/.

[34] "Corporate Control of Food" (accessed June 19, 2022), Greenpeace,
www.greenpeace.org/usa/sustainable-agriculture/issues/corporate
-control/.

[35] James Temple, "Bill Gates: Rich Nations Should Shift Entirely to
Synthetic Beef," February 14, 2021, *MIT Technology Review*, www
.technologyreview.com/2021/02/14/1018296/bill-gates-climate
-change-beef-trees-microsoft/.

[36] Chris Young, "Bill Gates New Meat Alternative is Made Out of
a Volcanic Microbe," July 5, 2021, *Interesting Engineering*, www
.interestingengineering.com/bill-gates-backed-new-meat-alternative
-is-made-out-of-a-volcanic-microbe.

[37] Sandee Lamotte, "The Food that Can Feed, and Maybe Save the
Planet: Bugs," October 25, 2019, *CNN*, www.cnn.com/2019/10/25
/health/insects-feed-save-planet-wellness/index.html.

## Chapter Nine

[1] Klaus Schwab, *Stakeholder Capitalism: A Global Economy that Works
for Progress, People and the Planet* (Hoboken, New Jersey, John H.
Wiley & Sons, January 27, 2021), p. i.

[2] Ibid.

[3] Ibid. at p. ii.

[4] Ibid. at p. xv.

[5] Ibid. at p. 56.

[6]  Ibid. at p. 57.

[7]  Ibid. at p. 233.

[8]  Ibid. at p. 144.

[9]  Ibid. at p. 147.

[10]  Ibid.

[11]  Ibid. at p. 225.

[12]  Klaus Schwab and Thierry Mallert, *The Great Narrative for a Better Future* (Geneva, Switzerland, Forum Publishing, 2022), p. 19.

[13]  Ibid. at p. 146.

[14]  Ibid.

[15]  Ibid. at p. 158.

[16]  Ibid. at p. 160.

[17]  Augustine of Hippo (accessed June 19, 2022), Good-Reads – Quotable Quotes, www.goodreads.com/quotes/798196-the-truth-is -like-a-lion-you-don-t-have-to.

## Chapter Ten

[1]  Vigilant Citizen, "The Top 10 Creepiest & Most Dystopian Things Pushed By The World Economic Forum," June 4, 2022, *Newswars*, www.newswars.com/the-top-10-creepiest-most-dystopian-things -pushed-by-the-world-economic-forum/.

[2]  "Flashback: Great Reset Architect Klaus Schwab Brags WEF 'Penetrates' Cabinets of World Leaders," January 26, 2022, *Newswars*, www.newswars.com/flashback-great-reset-architect-klaus-schwab -brags-wef-penetrates-cabinets-of-world-leaders/.

[3]  R. Douglas Fields, "Mind Reading and Mind Control Technologies are Coming," March 10, 2022, *Scientific American*, www.blogs .scientificamerican.com/observations/mind-reading-and-mind -control-technologies-are-coming/.

[4]  Roman Balmakov, "Facts Matter: Top 9 Most Dystopian Things Pushed by the World Economic Forum," June 7, 2022, *Epoch TV*, www .theepochtimes.com/facts-matter-june-7-top-9-most-dystopian-things -pushed-by-the-world-economic-forum/.

5   Parwinder Sandhu, "Pfizer CEO Albert Bourla Admits to Presence
    of Biological Chip in Vaccines? Viral Video Fuels 'Microchip'
    Conspiracy Theory," December 18, 2021, *International Business Times*,
    www.ibtimes.sg/pfizer-ceo-albert-bourla-admits-presence-biological
    -chip-vaccines-viral-video-fuels-61857.
6   "World Economic Forum Deleted Video: Lockdowns are Improving
    Cities Around the World," February 27, 2021, *You Tube*, www.youtube
    .com/watch?v=fb6U8xkn8jM.
7   Vigilant Citizen, "The Top 10 Creepiest & Most Dystopian Things
    Pushed By The World Economic Forum," June 4, 2022, *Newswars*,
    www.newswars.com/the-top-10-creepiest-most-dystopian-things
    -pushed-by-the-world-economic-forum/.
8   Andrea Willage, "What are the Long-term Effects of the COVID-19
    Pandemic? These 5 Trends Give Us a Glimpse," August 11, 2021,
    World Economic Forum, www.weforum.org/agenda/2021/08
    /covid19-long-term-effects-society-digital/.
9   Vigilant Citizen, "What is the Great Reset?: A Blatant Propaganda
    Video by the World Economic Forum," February 2, 2021, *The
    Vigilant Citizen*, www.vigilantcitizen.com/latestnews/what-is-the
    -great-reset-a-blatant-propaganda-video-by-the-world-economic
    -forum/.
10  Joshua Klein, "World Economic Forum" Australia's Esafety
    Commissioner Calls for 'Recalibration' of Human Rights, Free Speech,"
    May 24, 2022, *Breitbart*, www.breitbart.com/politics/2022/05/24
    /world-economic-forum-australias-esafety-commissioner-calls-for
    -recalibration-of-human-rights-free-speech/.
11  "Your Clothing Would be Tracked Soon," December 9, 2021,
    *You Tube*, www.youtube.com/watch?v=h8SWY6_b67A.
12  "World Economic Forum: Smartphones Will Be in Your Body
    by 2030," May 27, 2022, *You Tube*, www.youtube.com/watch?v
    =LJpBJAHqY0M.
13  World Economic Forum, *Twitter*, December 27, 2016, 2:09 p.m.,
    www.twitter.com/wef/status/813869325635424256?lang=en.

14 Ceri Parker, "8 Predictions for the World in 2030," November 12, 2016, *World Economic Forum*, www.weforum.org/agenda/2016/11/8-predictions-for-the-world-in-2030/.

15 *The New American Bible, Book of John*, Chap. 1, 5 (Nashville, Tennessee, Thomas Nelson, 1987), p. 1189.

# About the Author

B orn and raised in Texas, **Alex Jones** cuts through the lies of the globalists' official narrative with unrivaled analysis that has simultaneously led to him becoming the most talked about AND the most censored name in broadcasting.

Jones has indisputably left his mark on popular culture and has influenced many political and prominent figures in the industry. Wielding the slogan "There is a war on for your mind," Jones challenges big media with his daily broadcast of *The Alex Jones Show* by covering news the architects of the Great Reset want to be kept hidden.

But lately, due to his discernment repeatedly being vindicated, the fan-created phrase "Alex Jones was right" may now be the most iconic line associated with the radio host.

From the roots of his public-access show in Austin, Texas in the '90s, to now running and operating his own media empire with over 400 radio and cable/television stations, hundreds of online streaming platforms, and international syndication, Jones' wildly-popular *Infowars* has proven itself to be a powerful counter to the corporate-owned mainstream media.

Jones built *Infowars* from the ground up by putting profits back into the company. The listeners and viewers are Alex's partners, and he has vowed to honor their trust and always remain truly independent.

Daily, on his titular radio broadcast, Jones connects the dots and digs deeper into the story—often with the insight of experts, whistleblowers and insiders—to seek the truth and expose the scientifically engineered lies of the globalists and their ultimate goal of enslaving humanity.

Jones defined globalists and their mission during a recent edition of *The Alex Jones Show*: "A globalist is a member of the global-corporate combine that is attempting to establish an authoritarian world government, whose eventual aim of world government is to be able to carry out a transhumanist revolution that results in the death of the vast majority of the world population and, out of that cataclysm, a new super race."

Jones uses his production to reach as many hearts and minds as possible, because he believes that by informing people about the true nature of power, we can foster a real debate about humanity's destiny, and allow the species to evolve toward a more orderly singularity, that has humans at the core of a system, which is based around maintaining free will and integrity. This defies the transhumanist goal of Social Darwinism and scientific dictatorship.

Jones is internationally recognized as a trailblazer of new media and an icon of the Great Awakening and the pro-liberty movement.

"Alex Jones is a model for people to create their own media," Michael Harrison, editor of the industry trade magazine *Talkers*, told *Rolling Stone* writer Alexander Zaitchik. "When the history is written of talk broadcasting's transition from the corporate model of the 20th century to the digital, independent model of the 21st century, he will be considered an early trailblazer."

Additionally, Jones is an accomplished filmmaker who has produced many works since his first documentary, *America: Destroyed By Design*, was released in 1997. His seminal film, *Endgame: Blueprint For Global Enslavement* (2007), is more important now than ever before.

Also, Jones had a cameo role in Richard Linklater's *Waking Life*, a part that received a standing ovation at the Sundance Film Festival. He also appeared as the "street prophet" in Linklater's 2006 film, *A Scanner Darkly*, based on the novel of the same name by Philip K. Dick.

"Alex's mind is a turbocharged research and information processor, and he's a really gifted, articulate communicator," director Linklater once said. "Most people struggle to articulate all the swirling over-abundance of information out there and aren't that passionate about anything, but Alex pulls it all together for a lot of people."

Indeed, Alex Jones possesses three traits globalists have worked tirelessly to stamp out of the masses in order to create a permanent underclass: being well-read, having a good memory, and caring about others.

# Acknowledgments

I could not have remained in this fight if not for the unwavering support of my family through the years. From the bottom of my heart, thank you. I love you.

I would like to thank all our predecessors in this timeless struggle for human liberty. We are all indebted to those who came before us, the ancestors, the pioneers who fought and died for freedom, for a dream that we know today as western civilization. We are the blessed inheritors of that dream, but only if we succeed in defending it against the assaults of the modern age.

Thank you to everyone currently involved in the effort to preserve classic western values and a classical liberal system against the insidious influences of technofascism and neo-globalism. We are facing a powerful enemy, almost too powerful to comprehend. The very soul of America as we know it is falling victim to a takeover, a coup d'état. Our beautiful land is captured and polluted by factory farms, our treasured schools poisoned with technocratic ideologies disguised as truths, and our constitutional rights jeopardized by apocalyptic new policies that take aim at the essence of western democracy. The human mind and heart are turned into corporate commodities to be manipulated and used in the pursuit of inconceivable concentrations of power. But worst of all, these are not uniquely American threats. The target of the takeover is the whole world.

Yet we must believe, if we are to continue, in the capacity of the human spirit to transcend even those obstacles that seem insurmountable, and to triumph over even those enemies that seem too determined, too powerful to ever be vanquished. But have no fear. We have seen it in every culture and context; ultimately, the deep-rooted human urge toward freedom will always prevail over the lesser urges of greed on the one hand and fear on the other. This is a long-term struggle to build a better world for our children. Thank you for joining me in these pages, for opening your mind to a terrifying reality, for resisting the myriad forces that seek to control what you think and read, for standing up against the almost endless propaganda and censorship. I hope you will continue to resist; for America and for all of humanity.

Finally, I'd like to thank writer extraordinaire, Kent Heckenlively. I am deeply grateful for his help in condensing and organizing the research presented here and look forward to working with him on future projects.